I want to thank several dancers who made this book possible:

Mary Thrasher and Rosemary Wolfe for
choreographing content and instructional strategies...

Therese Palmertree and her staff from
McComb, Mississippi who provided a unique dance floor...

My children and grandchildren who give me
a reason to keep dancing...

And most of all, Cynthia, who for the past 42 years has made
every moment a dance in the spaces between the notes.

Copyright © 2012 Triple-C-21

All rights reserved.

ISBN-10: 061561681X

EAN-13: 9780615616810

MATH AND THE MIDDLE SCHOOL DANCE

DIGITIZING INSTRUCTIONAL ROUTINES TO MAXIMIZE ENTREPRENEURIAL THINKING

DR. DAN JOHNSON

TRIPLE-C-21, LLC

Foreward

This dance is dedicated to Joe Jabaily, a school board president who died as he lived, leveling the playing field for others. One Sunday, as Joe was riding in a charity triathlon, he was struck by a car and killed. Delivering his eulogy was one of the most difficult yet transformative experiences of my life.

Joe was a neurologist who was more comfortable with a crowd at a Grateful Dead concert than with a group of Rotarians. He was a spiritual man with no church affiliation—as popular with senior citizens as with young adults. His youngest son poignantly captured Joe's essence when he said, "Dad could dance in the spaces between the notes."

At the time, those words signified the uniqueness of Joe's personality and the uniqueness of our relationship. It was several years later that I realized why this dance metaphor kept playing in my head. Joe and I had been social coconspirators—educational entrepreneurs walking the wrong way in the middle of a Macy's parade—an irritant to the marchers and little more than a distraction to many spectators.

Now that I'm a semi-retired consultant, I spend less time marching from point A to point B. Instead, I focus on teaching and learning as a dance in the spaces between the notes, where entrepreneurs transform content into ideas and ideas into action. One afternoon, as I was wrapping up a workshop about dancing in the spaces, I noticed a small group of administrators still sitting at a table. A principal from their group called out, "Dr. Dan, can we talk for a moment about the dance?"

Everyone at her table chuckled, and I didn't know what to expect as I approached the group. We chatted for a few minutes, and then someone said, "You've changed the conversation at this table. I can speak for our entire group when I say we'll never think of school reform in the same way again. You should write a book about dancing in the spaces between the notes so this conversation can be expanded to more schools."

This is the book. Its content doesn't fit into a neat little package of logical sequential steps. In fact, I hope *Math and the Middle School Dance* turns your logical sequential ideas about teaching and learning upside down. I hope it causes you to rethink the purpose of education and your role in the change process, that it gives you a reason to be optimistic about the future of education and the future of our democracy. Whether you're a student, a teacher, a parent, or an interested citizen, I hope you'll become the catalyst for transforming your school's logical sequential march into a dynamic and productive *dance in the spaces between the notes.*

Contents

Introduction — xi

PART I — Dancing in the Spaces between the Notes — 1
How Kids Think and Why it Matters
Smart Looks Different at a Dance — 3
Is Being Smart a Matter of DNA?
Focus on Differences—Not Deficiencies — 23
Does Practice Make Perfect?
I Can Dance — 43
Is Critical Thinking the Key to Success?

PART II — Mastering the Digital Two-Step — 63
Managing an Entrepreneurial Culture
Reach Back—Teach Forward — 65
Are Thinking Skills More Important than Content?

Choreographing the Dance	87
Don't All Good Teachers Teach Critical Thinking?	
Producing a Dance Culture	111
Can We Evaluate Entrepreneurial Thinking?	
Conclusion	133
Resources	141
References	145
Index	149

Introduction

If a man does not keep pace with his companions, perhaps it is because he hears a different drummer. Let him step to the music he hears, however measured or far away.
—Thoreau

Math and the Middle School Dance is about *entrepreneurial thinking*. For many years education has been a parade from point A to point B. We have Common Core standards to ensure that all students march in the same general direction as their classmates. We have standardized tests to identify flaws in their marching routines. The problem is that today's students aren't very excited about marching, and the public has grown weary of the parade.

My purpose in writing this book is to question several core assumptions underlying this parade mentality. I've focused on grades 5 through 9 because I've been a middle school teacher, principal, parent, and grandparent. I've also spent almost 20 years as a school superintendent comparing middle school students with their elementary and high school counterparts. In case there's any doubt, let me assure you that middle school students are unique.

First, unlike elementary students, middle school students realize adults don't know as much as we think we know. However, unlike high school students, they haven't learned what happens to students who question our authority.

As adults, we assume we know better than students what success looks like. We assume that if students are successful in school, they'll be successful in life. So, after they practice certain routines for 13 years and endure various tests and competitions, we parade them across a stage in front of their parents and the public and certify them as educated citizens.

Realizing that such parades can be costly, we've added more money to school budgets to train our teachers and school administrators. We've increased practice time for students and added high stakes testing to increase competition. Yet, over the past several years, US students haven't performed as successfully in science and math as students from other industrialized countries.

Since we know how education should work, or at least assume we know, we've concluded that US students lack the drive necessary to be successful in an increasingly competitive world. We've concluded that an emphasis on science, technology, engineering, and math (STEM) can improve their thinking and increase their interest in school. So, we're organizing STEM parades driven by the digital drumbeat of data analysis.

We know from observing students that they love their digital toys. We've also seen how digital technology increases the volume and availability of information. It allows educators to manage the data we need to identify students' academic deficits. We hope that if we identify students' deficits early and often, we can help them keep in step with their international peers. At the very least, we should be able to encourage our best and brightest students to excel—right?

Well, *not exactly*—it seems that even what we consider to be our best and brightest students are falling behind their international peers. We work hard to improve standards and assessments, at getting students to practice what we want them to learn, and at updating our instructional routines. We assume all students want to march in our parade, or can at least become reasonably proficient at marching. But what does it mean when even the best and brightest US students are falling behind? Is it time to question our assumptions about education as a march from point A to point B?

The answers to these questions may lie somewhere in the middle, in grades 5 through 9, where it seems students prefer dancing to marching. During the middle school years, students' brains begin to develop the connections they need to make their own judgments. While these new brain cells won't be fully developed until students reach their early twenties, they place students in an awkward position. They have the ability to see mistakes in our thinking, but they lack the means to do much about it. They're caught between the concrete world of childhood and the abstract world of adulthood.

If we expect students to use what they've learned from elementary school as a path to high school graduation, we have to understand what's happening in middle school. When we understand this, we may understand the importance of adaptive thinking over regimented behaviors. We may understand the importance of teaching entrepreneurial thinking. As Warren Bennis (1989) suggests, we lead not simply by doing things right, but by doing the right things.

We have to become educational entrepreneurs, willing to transform our mistakes into learning opportunities. An entrepreneur's work is messy at times. It exists in a world that isn't exactly as logical or sequential as our textbooks, Common Core standards, and standardized tests might lead us to believe. But entrepreneurial thinking involves much more than taking risks. Successful entrepreneurs *manage* risks. As educators, we can't help students become entrepreneurs until we improve our ability to organize, manage, and assume the risks associated with learning in a changing world.

Grades 5-9 provide a breeding ground for risk. Middle school students have more opportunities to make choices than they had in elementary school. Yet, they lack the judgment necessary to understand the full impact of their decisions on themselves and on those around them. We can help them learn to manage

Introduction

these risks—to find personal satisfaction in creating marketable products.

Imagine what would happen if students understood that their intellectual capacity is one of the most valuable products they'll ever create. Imagine if every day of school involved a life lesson in identifying, articulating, and solving meaningful problems. What might happen if students could take a little less time to focus on our answers and a little more to focus on their questions? What might happen if teachers could use digital technology to manage instructional routines so they could focus on how students learn? What might happen if, instead of focusing on students' deficits, we focused on their strengths? Could we transform students' innate talents into marketable intellectual strengths?

Common Core standards, standardized tests, and hard work are important pieces of the educational puzzle. We have to help students see the patterns among these pieces. To accomplish this, we have to do a better job of assessing how our thinking impacts their thinking. It's important for students to know how the world measures success. But it's equally important for them to build their own measures of success by struggling with ambiguity across multiple learning experiences.

Computer processors are wired to accept yes or no responses. Our brains are wired to explore the nuances between yes and no—the spaces between point A and point B. By the time students reach grade 5, they've experienced few opportunities to question teachers' assumptions, let alone question their own.

Life in a democracy requires that we teach students to manage risk—not avoid it.

Throughout this book we'll focus on learning as a process of questioning assumptions. But instead of answering these questions with a *yes or no*, we'll explore what happens when the answers fall in the spaces between yes and no. In part 1, we'll question three seemingly opposing, but not mutually exclusive, assumptions about learning. We'll see if our answers to the following questions suggest a different way of managing educational experiences.

1. Is being smart a matter of DNA?

2. Does practice make perfect?

3. Is critical thinking the key to success?

In part 2, we'll consider how we can use digital technology to manage instructional routines so we have more time to explore how our assumptions impact students' learning. Our answers to these three questions about learning affect how we teach and ultimately how we create an entrepreneurial culture within our schools. The questions driving these teaching and leadership assumptions look like this.

4. Are thinking skills more important than content?

5. Don't all good teachers teach critical thinking?

6. Can we evaluate entrepreneurial thinking?

INTRODUCTION

Our answers to this second set of questions will suggest implications for education beyond the middle school years. If we understand what students need to navigate grades 5 through 9, we may make better decisions about how we manage learning prior to and following those years.

As we explore these questions in a middle school setting, we'll consider examples of thinking tools (including digital technology) that we can use to transform schools into entrepreneurial centers. But we'll avoid describing a litany of tools that might overshadow the transformation process itself. The partial list of thinking tools and services at the end of this book offers a starting point for creating even better entrepreneurial tools.

I've also encouraged several *entrepreneurs* to create user friendly reference books for aspiring dancers who want to refine specific entrepreneurial skills. These reference books will address individual topics such as curriculum alignment with Common Core standards, practical applications of classroom thinking tools, self efficacy in daily practice, managing technology across content areas, planning meetings to build a capacity for critical thinking, aligning evaluation with systemic values, and entrepreneurial thinking in minority schools.

If we are to teach students to *dance in the spaces between the notes* represented by Common Core standards and standardized tests, we need to rethink how we choreograph the dance. Entrepreneurs don't ignore existing products and services. They study them in multiple combinations. They don't blindly follow routines. They question them as a means of developing a better product.

As educators, we need to become entrepreneurs willing to dance in the spaces between Common Core standards and standardized test results. These are the spaces where critical thinking and self efficacy determine what students can create with our guidance and support. We need to pursue the question, "What do those Common Core standards look like in the classroom, and how can we create schools that transform standards into a marketable intellectual product?"

PART I

DANCING IN THE SPACES
BETWEEN THE NOTES:

HOW KIDS THINK AND WHY IT MATTERS

Smart Looks Different at a Dance

Is Being Smart a Matter of DNA?

You haven't lived until you've chaperoned a middle school dance. It starts with the student council president asking for a meeting with the principal.

"Mr. Chang, the kids want to have a dance."

"Why don't we just hold a relay race after school? I spent most of my time at the last dance corralling runners."

"Oh, come on, Mr. Chang. That was just a few sixth graders."

"Well, then there was Bobby practicing his mouth-to-mouth resuscitation skills. Tanya's mother still hasn't recovered from that experience."

"Mr. Chang, be serious."

"Okay, let's start with sponsors."

"Mrs. G. said she would sponsor it, and Mr. Frank said maybe."

Of course, Mr. Chang knows that two sponsors won't be adequate for a middle school dance. He'll need at least one willing to teach the shy kids some dance steps, one to monitor the darker corners of the dance floor, and one to monitor the runners. He'll need to twist some arms of *cool* teachers or parents—cool, but not too cool.

Cool means they'll teach reluctant kids to dance. They won't freak out when they realize several eighth-grade students not only know what a French kiss is, but also are trying to refine it into an art form. Too cool means they're willing to let middle school kids *have their fun* when many parents wish elementary school extended all the way to high school.

These are the kids we expect to learn math. And trust me; they're much more interested in what happens at the dance than in what happens in our classrooms. They have more hormones than brains, and they haven't learned to manage either very effectively. Face it, school isn't their top priority, and math doesn't top their list of favorite subjects.

People who teach math probably like it, or at least they're reasonably good at it. Students have no choice in the matter. So, we shouldn't assume that anyone who doesn't share our enthusiasm for math is either lazy or dumb. Have you ever wondered what would happen if, as adults, we began our educational planning with a different set of assumptions about learning?

Instead of starting with what students should know and be able to do, we might first ask whether we believe all students can learn. We might ask if we've taught students to manage more than books and assignments. We might also ask if we've taught them to think critically and to manage their own learning, even when they have no interest in the content.

When we start the conversation by asking what we want students to know and be able to do in math, we assume learning math is a logical sequential training process based on content. We're assuming that what separates successful math students from unsuccessful math students is natural talent, hard work, paying attention, and following directions. Either we believe students are born with certain intellectual limits, or we believe they can do anything they want if they're willing to work hard enough. When we give students feedback, we say, "We believe you can succeed if you try harder." The students hear, "If I didn't get this, I'm either dumb or lazy. Oh well, I'd rather be at the dance."

Students don't come to grades 5-9 with a full range of life experiences. They're struggling with a desire to be like an adult idol, with a need to fit in with friends, and with a fear of being themselves—whatever that might be. They haven't developed the ability to distinguish between intentions and actions. They don't have the ability to separate their performance in a particular situation from who they are as a person.

Learning at this age is not as logical or sequential as our math curriculum suggests. Sometimes hard work doesn't pay off. Sometimes no matter how focused or self-disciplined students try to be, they don't have the confidence or the experiential background necessary to accomplish certain things—at least not to our specifications.

Learning math in grades 5-9 isn't a logical sequential march from knowledge acquisition to knowledge application. Adults are asking students from ten to fifteen years of age to *grow up*. The students are saying, "I can't grow-up if you make all my decisions for me. I can make some of my own decisions, you know."

The world of adolescence is filtered through a fuzzy lens. A new set of hormones clouds a new and unfocused set of brain cells. No matter how understanding or dedicated we may be as educators, it isn't easy to compete with these distractions. It isn't easy to remember that middle school students are often struggling just as hard as we are to deal with them. Schools would be easier to manage if kids thought the way adults think. But they don't. They don't even think the way other kids think.

Is Being Smart a Matter of DNA?

Meet the Student Dancers

Hi, I'm Tom. My mom still calls me Tommy. I'm nervous about starting middle school—mostly about math. Mrs. Beck—that's my fifth-grade teacher—says math in middle school will be tough. She says if I work hard enough, I may be ready for algebra by eighth grade. Don't know if I want to take algebra in eighth grade, but that's what all the smart kids do.

All my teachers say I'm smart and responsible. I work hard, but Mrs. Beck told my mom I should get a math tutor this summer. She says I need to work on word problems. I'm good at fractions and decimals, but those word problems don't make sense to me. I get math when Mrs. Beck explains the word problems.

I want to be an engineer like my dad, so I guess I need math. I asked my mom to schedule the tutoring as soon as school's out to get it over with. I want to play ball and go to camp with my friends too. Well, I better get started on my homework. I have to get it done before I'm allowed to surf the net. Nice talking to you.

I'm Juan. I sit next to Tommy in class. Sometimes Mrs. Beck puts us in math groups, and I work with Tommy. He's smarter than I

am. Mrs. Beck says that's because he pays attention and works hard. She likes me too though—says I can do good work but I'm too careless. Mrs. Beck told my mom middle school can be a new start for me. I hope so.

Sometimes I just get really depressed. You know, it's hard trying to keep up with kids like Tommy and Lakya. Lakya is so smart she can ace every test and still have time to have fun. Mrs. Beck tells her she needs to be more self-disciplined. If I wasn't a boy though, I'd hang out with her. She's so cool, not like most girls.

Anyhow, my biggest worry about middle school is having time for friends. I'm glad my counselor told my mom I need time for friends. All Mom worries about is my schoolwork, especially math. She says she wasn't good at math, and she wants me to do better. Mrs. Beck tells us we can do anything we want if we just work hard enough.

Right now I don't know what I want to do when I grow up. I don't even know what I want to do next week except be with my friends and ride my horse. That's when I'm happiest—when I'm with Jake and my friends. They accept me for who I am. Oh well, maybe Mom and Mrs. Beck and my counselor are right. Maybe things will get better next year.

Hi, I'm Lakya. I don't know what you want me to tell you. I do fine in school, but it's a bore. I'm not afraid of middle school. I'm the best math student in my class—better than Tom. He gets better grades sometimes, but that's because he's the teacher's pet.

Tom never forgets to do his homework or gets yelled at for reading a book in math class. I know I should do my homework, but there's one thing I don't get: why do I have to do homework if I can already ace all my tests?

Is Being Smart a Matter of DNA?

Mrs. Beck didn't like it when I argued with her about practice making perfect. I said practice didn't make perfect for me. I just get math. It's fun to solve those word problems. But she says I'll be sorry when I get to middle school—I need to be more responsible and self-disciplined. She says middle school teachers won't be as patient as she is. She told my mom and dad I would flunk middle school math if I didn't learn to keep an organized notebook.

I guess life is about rules as long as you're a kid. It just doesn't make sense to me. Don't get me wrong. I like Mrs. Beck. She's just old—thirty-six or something, I think. She's not as old as my parents, but I have to show all of them how to program their phones, run the computer for math class, and all that technical stuff.

I want to work with computers when I grow up, so I have to have math. Dad's going to explain some computer programming to me this summer. He wants me to get back into the gifted class in middle school—says my programming skills ought to impress them. Wish I could go to work with my dad instead of going to middle school. At least they have a lab at the middle school—not as cool as Dad's lab, but cool.

Hey, I'm Jamal. Let me catch my breath. I just set a new track record in gym class—kicked butt. Whew, I wish I could spend all day in gym class. Mrs. Beck says I don't pay attention in class, but math just isn't fun like gym. I try to pay attention like my mom wants me to. I really do. But I get distracted. Like I get distracted when Lakya tells a joke or when she's brushing her hair. She's beautiful. Mostly, I just get really tired of sitting. School's boring.

Mrs. Beck says I could do better if I sat still and paid attention. She says I don't work hard enough, but Coach B. says I'm the hardest worker he ever saw. He says I could be the next Jim Thorpe—this Native American guy that ticked off Hitler when he beat all the Germans in track.

Coach gave me that book, but Mrs. Beck said we weren't learning about Hitler this year. She let me read the book in silent reading time, but she got tired of me talking about it. She said I needed to spend more time on math and English and less time on sports.

Mrs. Beck told my mom she likes me. She said she thinks I lost out because we've moved from school to school so much. She said she thinks I need a male figure in my life, since my dad doesn't live with my mom and me.

When my mom told me Mrs. Beck liked me, I thought things would be different at school. I really tried to do better, but I don't get fractions and decimals and all that other stuff. I wish math was more about percentages. I can do percentages when I figure averages for Coach B.

Well, I better go. I'll get in trouble if I don't find my math homework.

These are only four of the students Ms. Toffler will face in her sixth-grade math classes next year. Each of the other twenty students in this class, along with one hundred students in four additional classes, will pose an equally unique set of challenges. Ms. Toffler is a third-year teacher who has recently completed her master's degree in instructional technology. She hopes to use technology more effectively to meet her students' individual needs. Teaching adolescents presents some interesting challenges, and Ms. Toffler is determined to be a teacher who makes a positive difference in her students' lives.

Meet the Dance Instructor

Hi, I'm Ms. Toffler—Gloria. Welcome to my chaotic life. I'm not complaining. I'm one of the lucky teachers who managed to keep my job during the recent budget cuts. I guess I thought my fourth year of teaching would be different. Earning my master's degree in instructional technology wasn't easy for me as a single mom. But my ex helped with my daughter. I have to give him that.

I had all these great ideas for next year—what I could do with everything I learned in graduate school about how kids' brains work in a math classroom. Then there would be all the cool stuff I could download from the Internet to make math come alive. Now the good life has seemed to become more about staying alive. Oh no, did I just use the name of a disco song? That was my mother's era.

Really, I love my job. But I also love being a mom. And I'm trying to get my life back together after a difficult divorce. Each day I have to get Ellie off to school. She's a gem, handling the divorce really well, according to her counselor. Ellie also does really well at school. I don't have to miss work to deal with her problems the way some parents do.

After school is sometimes a bit of a hassle. I have department meetings and professional learning community sessions. Some nights my teammate and I need to talk about students or plan a unit together. The Skype camera my parents bought me should eliminate one meeting by letting me plan with my partner electronically after Ellie goes to bed.

It's a good thing my parents live close by and are retired. Mom picks up Ellie when I have meetings. On those nights, Ellie and I have dinner at Mom's house before we go home. During our commute, I listen to the events of Ellie's day. On days when I haven't had a meeting, we fix a snack, and I get Ellie started on her homework. After dinner I spend two more hours on my schoolwork—correcting papers and preparing for the next day's classes.

I'm not complaining. I'm a lucky person—luckier than friends who have lost their jobs or don't live close to their parents. I just get down sometimes, overwhelmed. When I got married and started work as an engineer, I thought I had achieved the American dream. After Ellie was born, my ex and I decided I would take a couple of years off to be a stay-at-home mom. When he didn't get the promotion we expected, I had to go back to work. I got my teaching degree, and then things went south between us.

So here I am. I love my daughter, I love my job, and I loved graduate school. Somewhere in all of this chaos, there's a life, I think. At least that's what my principal, Mr. Chang, tells me.

Meet the Producer

Hi, I'm Ron Chang. I like to say that my job as principal is to protect my teachers from the wolves—the parents and central office folks. Last spring I worked with my staff to put together a comprehensive action plan to improve math based on our test data. Now I'm trying to figure out the best way to let teachers know they won't be getting their new math materials this year, and their team planning time has been reduced to save dollars.

When I'm not doing that, I'm explaining to parents that the budget cuts won't be the end of the world. Several of my most active parents have moved for work reasons. Others can't commit more time to supporting the school because of increased demands at work.

Thanks to the superintendent's commitment to technology, my school will still receive the computers, software, and other digital equipment we were promised last spring. But I'll have to convince the staff to attend after-school professional development, with little or no chance of pay, so they can learn how to use the new software and equipment.

Many of my classrooms are equipped with the latest educational technology, from computers to interactive smartboards. Computers have replaced pencils and paper, interactive electronic boards have replaced chalkboards and whiteboards, and Internet videos have replaced filmstrips and movies. But much more change will be required before we see a difference in student performance.

My teachers were making progress toward teaching students to summarize information, to compare and contrast, and to develop other strategies that lead to academic success. They actually enjoyed working in professional learning communities, studying Marzano, Paul and Elder, and other critical thinking researchers. But the recent budget cuts have almost destroyed their morale.

I've tried to convince people that our work is more like dancing than running a race. We take a few steps forward and then jog to one side. Occasionally, we have to move backward, but we have to keep dancing. I tell my math teachers like Ms. Toffler that the old math standards are a waltz we play for kids who would rather hear hip-hop. The Common Core standards play a more current song, but we're still the ones responsible for helping our students interpret the music. I tell them David Keirsey's research on how people process information on a daily basis is similar to a middle school dance floor.

IS BEING SMART A MATTER OF DNA?

THE DANCE FLOOR

Math in grades 5-9 is like a middle school dance. Some kids have been studying the math dance for years. Others were apparently born dancers. Some would rather sit by the wall and talk with friends or run from one side of the dance floor to the other. Teachers and principals want to make the dance a success, but they have their hands full with their own set of issues.

The simple truth is that the world doesn't stop turning for students or educators to catch their breath. The music keeps playing whether or not anyone is dancing. It's not surprising that teachers ask, "So how can I learn to manage my math classroom in spite of this chaos?"

About 25 years ago, I found temperament to be a useful tool in addressing this question. Temperament doesn't account for every individual difference in people's behavior, but it helps us see patterns. These patterns provide a structure for recognizing and dealing with the human side of learning. Keirsey and Bates (1998) describe these patterns using terms like Idealist, Guardian, Rational, and Artisan. In the *Real Colors Homeowner's Guide* (Johnson 2004), I use colors in keeping with the National Curriculum and Training Institute approach to temperament (www.realcolors.org). I ask readers to think of temperament (the way we process information) in terms of a four-room house. For our purposes, I've shifted this analogy to a middle school dance floor as illustrated in figure 1.2.

Figure 1.2
The Dance Floor in Living Color

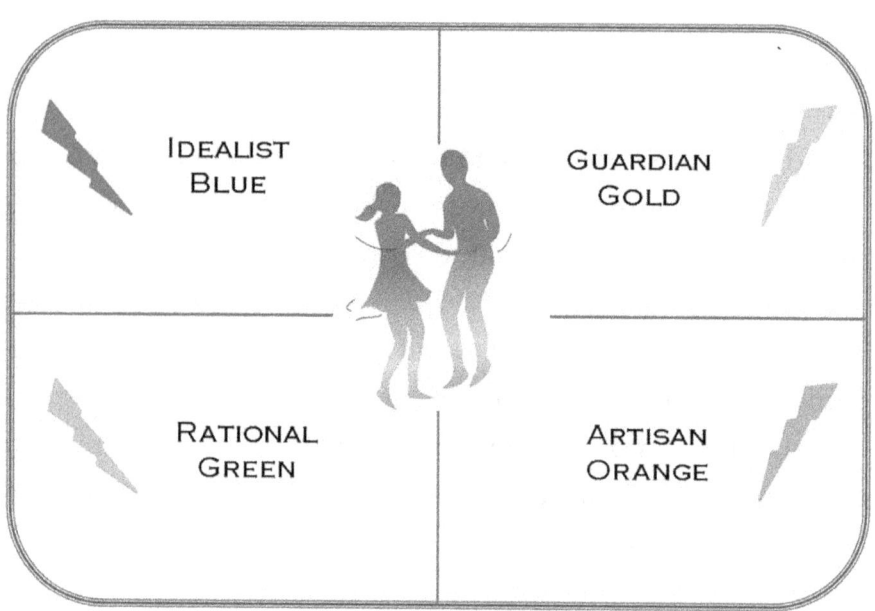

Think of the four areas of the dance floor as lenses through which teachers and students see the math dance. Each area of the dance floor (your brain) has an exterior lens linking you to the outside world. You can dance in all four areas of the floor, but you tend to dance in one area more than the other three. When you take math content onto the dance floor (mathematical thinking) you teach dancing the way you were taught to dance.

That's great for the students who learn the way their teachers teach. Tom, for example, pays attention and keeps copious notes. He's a teacher's dream student. But what happens to students whose information processing takes place in a different area of the dance floor? Figure 1.3 illustrates how differently people dance their way through life and learning.

Is Being Smart a Matter of DNA?

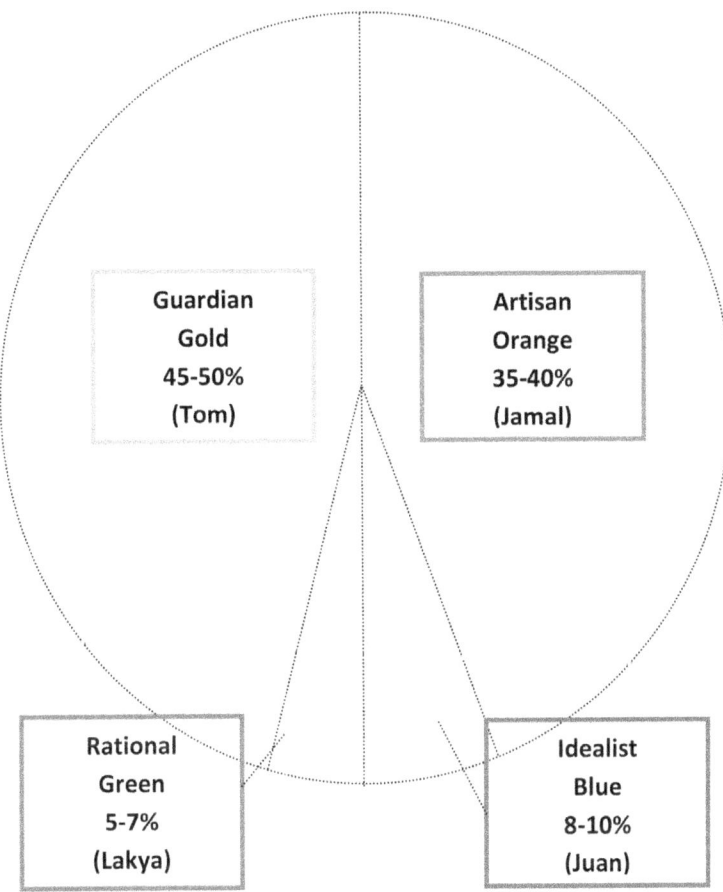

Figure 1.3
Temperament Distribution

According to Keirsey and Bates (www.keirsey.com), approximately 45 to 50 percent of the world processes information on the Guardian portion of the dance floor. In *Real Colors* terminology (www.realcolors.org) we refer to these individuals as Gold. The Guardian/Gold portion of the dance floor is where the Toms of our classrooms watch someone else dance and slowly try to mimic their steps. They learn one dance at a time until they perfect it. They welcome an opportunity to show others what they've learned and win their approval. *These Guardians/ Gold dancers spend so much time guarding their area of the dance floor that they have little time left to explore anything else.*

As figure 1.3 also illustrates, approximately 35 to 40 percent of the world processes information on the Artisan/Orange portion of the dance floor. Like Guardians, they watch and mimic. But when they demonstrate their moves, they generally include improvisation—not always an asset in a math classroom. *These are the Jamals of our classrooms, who often perform better in the gym or the band room where improvisation is honored.*

Notice that less than 20 percent of the dance floor is left for the Idealist/Blue and Rational/Green dancers. Roughly 8 to 10 percent of these dancers move on the Idealist/Blue portion of the floor. Like Juan, they process information in terms of how it affects them personally and how it improves their ability to connect with the world around them. They came to the dance to be with friends.

Finally, 5 to 7 percent of the dancers are sitting quietly along the wall, studying dance moves. These are the Rational/Greens, like Lakya, who analyze information carefully to determine how it fits with their own internal standards. They want to figure out how the dance works, but they have their own ideas about which dance is worth learning.

In terms of our math classrooms, this means that approximately 45 to 50 percent of our students (Guardian/Gold) feel comfortable with sequential routines and expectations. They see a purpose in drill and practice. The other students have difficulty with this sequential math march.

Jamal, who understands only about half of the math concepts being discussed, gets lost in thoughts about gym class. He represents the 35 to 40 percent of students in the Artisan/Orange area who have a difficult time maintaining focus and following complex explanations. They skip key steps in math procedures. When they practice, they practice an incomplete set of routines, which simply adds to their confusion.

Juan is lost between pleasing Ms. Toffler and pleasing his friends. He represents the 8 to 10 percent of the students in the Idealist/Blue area who are people pleasers. They're often as easily distracted as their Artisan/Orange classmates but less inclined to create problems for teachers. Their ability to see the world as others see it causes them to lose sight of their own needs and interests.

Lakya hears Ms. Toffler's words, but she may be thinking about their implications beyond the immediate lesson. She represents the 5 to 7 percent of the students (Rational/Green) who think about the implications of a math concept in multiple contexts. They get so engaged with the concept that they miss the directions for the practice assignment. They take incomplete notes and lose them. They do well on tests but don't complete their homework.

What figure 1.3 doesn't indicate is that two out of three teachers (65 to 70 percent) live and breathe the Guardian/Gold dance.

Their classrooms are organized around a singular focus, and success is based on mastering specific routines. Their teaching units are built around listening and memory and are driven by time and sequence. In short, their instruction favors Guardian/Gold learners and presents a risk for everyone else (about half the students in their classrooms).

By the time these students reach the middle grades (5-9), many have lost any hope of learning the math dance. They lack organizational skills that we try to remediate through note taking, gender separation, uniforms, or strict discipline procedures—if we don't mind damaging their entrepreneurial potential. Soon these students give up and are considered not only fidgety but lazy, unmotivated, and uncooperative.

So, is being smart a matter of DNA? *Not exactly*—if it were, why does the number of smart kids decrease by the time they reach middle school? In fact, research suggests that the number of struggling dancers actually increases throughout middle school and into high school. These students see themselves as *dumber* than their more obedient peers, and they see their side of the educational dance floor as disconnected and often isolated from the mainstream dance. Their only option is to take their dance elsewhere.

Eventually, even the Guardian/Gold dancers have trouble learning new dances. They forget some of the steps they've already *learned*. They don't realize that memorizing problem solving protocols for a test isn't the same thing as developing their own protocols. Memorizing so called basic skills doesn't guarantee they can apply those skills to algebra and other higher level math classes.

By the time students reach grade 5, the amount of knowledge they confront each day becomes too great to manage through rote memorization and practice. Even pneumonic devices used to recall isolated facts and algorithms prove too numerous to be of much help. Guardian/Gold students, who've learned to mimic teachers' dance steps in elementary school, become overwhelmed when they realize how many more dances they have to learn in middle school. As for everyone else, they begin to lose interest in the dance altogether.

No one intentionally choreographed this dance. No one set out to deceive anyone else. Life just seemed to unfold according to its own purpose and timeframe. So, if learning isn't simply a matter of DNA, is it possible that some students just need more time to practice? Let's keep dancing.

Focus on Differences— Not Deficiencies

Does Practice Make Perfect?

When you teach math, there are days when you feel as if you're only a few steps ahead of your students. People assume that because math teachers understand how math works, they can explain it to anyone. After all, if people pay attention and work hard, they can be anything they want to be. Don't you think if more kids were willing to work hard, anyone could learn math?

Figure 2.1
TIMSS Grade 8

Country	Average Score
Scale Average	500
Chinese Taipei	598
Korea, Rep. of	597
Singapore	593
Hong Kong	572
Japan	570
Hungary	517
England	513
Russian Federation	512
United States	508
Lithuania	506
Czech Republic	504

Not exactly—not everyone thrives on the Guardian/Gold portion of the dance floor, where math is taught as a sequence of dance steps to be mimicked. Let's examine why *more* content and *more* practice won't necessarily lead to *better* math results.

A March is not a Dance

Let's take a moment to consider what's driving the reform movement in math. Figure 2.1 illustrates recent international math scores for eighth-grade students (Trends in Mathematics and Science Study 1995-2010). Notice that US students score significantly lower than many of their peers worldwide. These findings have stimulated calls for significant reforms in US schools. We've spent several decades and billions of dollars training teachers how to teach mathematical concepts rather than simply teaching skills and algorithms. After all this investment, our students still aren't performing at a competitive international level.

Given these results and the current state of the US economy, is it any wonder we've fallen back on our mantra regarding hard work and sacrifice? Our kids have gone soft. Our schools have gone soft. Why, just look at the South Koreans. They have a longer school day and a longer school year. Most South Korean parents even send their kids to tutoring every day after school.

I understand this reaction, but I've also had a chance to observe the results of the South Korean system firsthand. In Seoul, where I spoke at a Global Education Forum, I had an opportunity to examine the South Korean system from several perspectives. At the forum I met with government leaders, educators, and businesspeople who were exploring how they could translate their success in math into economic and social opportunities for their citizens. I also made a point of visiting with students from elementary school through college. But my greatest insight came from my chance meeting with several high school students at the Korean National Museum.

My good friend and travel guide, Hemie, who was struggling to translate Korean history into English for me, asked these teenagers for help. They were quite willing to provide translations and were open to answering my questions about their school experiences. After enjoying their company through the museum walk, I bought the boys' lunch, and they began to talk more freely.

Kim, who spoke the most fluent English of the four, told me they were juniors in a South Korean high school. I learned that Kim had a B+ average. Yet, he described himself as not being smart enough to attend a top university in the US.

From the time Kim was an elementary school student, he had attended a private institute beyond the regular school day. Now in high school, he gets home from the private institute at 11:00 p.m. four nights a week. On Friday and Saturday nights, he studies at the library until after 1:00 a.m. in hopes of improving his grades and test scores. This is the life of a successful student in South Korea, a country that outperforms the rest of the world in math and has the world's highest per capita Internet usage.

What's wrong with this picture? The South Korean model runs counter to the entrepreneurial spirit that has made the US a beacon of hope for the world over the past one hundred years. We became a model of democracy because we refused to march in lockstep with European values. My conversations with Korean parents, educators, and business leaders reminded me that our greatness comes from entrepreneurship. We're dancers, not marchers.

> My conversations with Korean parents, educators, and business leaders reminded me that our greatness comes from entrepreneurship. We're dancers, not marchers.

As someone who has spent a lifetime as a school reformer, I've also come to the conclusion that the South Korean system of education is financially unsustainable. Kim's parents, like most middle class Korean parents, spend five hundred dollars per month to send Kim to a private institute. Like their US counterparts, many Korean parents struggle to keep pace. They're proud of their position as leaders in math and technology. But they're overwhelmed by the price they're paying for that success. They readily share their desire to understand the US penchant for creativity and entrepreneurial thinking.

There's nothing wrong with telling young people that learning requires hard work and sacrifice. But beyond hard work and self-discipline, learning requires an ability to strike a balance between our strengths and our liabilities as learners. Learning involves more than the good fortune to be born with a *learning gene*. We can teach students to listen, but we can also teach them to think critically and to interpret information according to their own strengths.

Rath (2007) suggests that our current attitude toward learning is based on the misguided maxim "You can be anything you want to be if you just try hard enough." He suggests that we should think more along the lines of, "You *cannot* be anything you want to be—but you *can* be a lot more of who you already are."

Critical thinking allows us to deal with the risks of balancing internal and external expectations. It allows us to tell our students, "You can become a lot more of who you are if you learn to balance your personal expectations with the expectations of those around you." Learning isn't synonymous with training. Math, like all content areas, is organized in a logical sequence of skills and concepts. But as we saw in the last chapter, only about half of us process the world in a logical sequential manner—Guardian/Gold and Rational/Green. The other half sees events as abstract and random. Logical sequential learners have an advantage in a classroom or lab, but abstract random learners often adapt more effectively to real-world demands.

So, what should mathematical reasoning look like in the classroom? What should students be doing? How should teachers manage the classroom? How should administrators manage the school to create a culture that supports mathematical reasoning?

THE GREEN SPACE ON THE DANCE FLOOR

Critical thinking is a rational process. It occurs on the Green portion of the dance floor. *The Elements of Critical Thinking* (Paul and Elder 2002) provides a structure for understanding this process. Take a moment to think about the eight elements of critical thinking as presented in figure 2.2.

Figure 2.2

Elements of Critical Thinking

1. **Purpose**—why are we learning this; or what concept is this problem/assignment addressing?
2. **Questions**—what is the nature of the specific question(s) being posed?
3. **Information**—what information do I need in order to answer this question?
4. **Inferences**—how did I come to my conclusions?
5. **Concepts**—what are the patterns imbedded in this problem that relate to a larger math concept?
6. **Assumptions**—what have I taken for granted?
7. **Implications**—what would a person conclude from my thinking?
8. **Point-of-view**—is my solution the only way to solve this problem?

Does Practice Make Perfect?

As you read through these elements, did you consider the extent to which you employ these skills in your learning? Did your teachers tell you about these elements of critical thinking? Did they model them for you? Did they require you to justify your problem solving procedures in terms of these or similar elements?

> *Most of us were trained to* do *math rather than to reason mathematically.*

Most of us were trained to *do* math rather than to reason mathematically. Our math teachers demonstrated mathematical algorithms and had us practice them until we could perform them automatically. The focus was on input and output rather than on reasoning—on the notes rather than on how we were navigating the spaces between the notes. We talked about process, but we didn't learn how to think mathematically. After all, it's difficult to know what another person is thinking. It's equally difficult to monitor our own thinking when we're trying to figure out what someone else wants. If only we could see students' thinking…

Well, we can. Wilhelm (2001) describes a think aloud as a process of making invisible mental processes visible to students and teachers. Getting students into the habit of thinking out loud enriches classroom interaction and provides teachers with an important diagnostic tool for learning. Instead of focusing on students' answers, teachers can focus on how they got to their answers.

In preparing for a think aloud, Ms. Toffler could consider the following. As you read these steps, think about where they fit within the eight elements of critical thinking.

- ✓ Purpose: What thinking needs to take place during this task (summarizing, sequencing, comparison-contrast, etc.)?
- ✓ Input: Students make predictions or create a hypothesis.

  They describe a mental picture they "see."

  They demonstrate how they connected the information with prior knowledge.

  Some students may benefit from creating an analogy: It is like…

  Ultimately, students verbalize obstacles so they can repair and refine their problem solving strategies.
- ✓ Modeling: Ms. Toffler can model the think aloud, showing students how to verbalize their thinking by completing starter phrases like these:
  - So far, I've learned…
  - This made me think of…
  - That didn't make sense…
  - I think ___ will happen next…
  - I reread that part because…
  - I was confused by…
  - I think the most important part was…
  - That is interesting because…
  - I wonder why…
  - I just thought of…
- ✓ Guided practice: Students demonstrate a think aloud.

- ✓ Checking for understanding: Ms. Toffler asks clarifying questions (described later).

- ✓ Independent practice: Groups of students assume thinker/questioner roles to correct a problem solution.

- ✓ Closure: Students describe key concepts in their own words.

You can think of the elements of critical thinking and these think aloud steps as cheat sheets that help teachers see the math dance from the students' perspectives. Let's consider how this think aloud process might look in Ms. Toffler's classroom. Remember, Ms. Toffler's strength is dancing on the Guardian/Gold portion of the floor. Critical thinking thrives on Rational/Green portion of the floor. Can you remember where her students dance?

EMPATHY AS THE PATHWAY TO DIFFERENTIATION

Empathy is not the same thing as sympathy. Teachers who have sympathy for struggling students feel their pain. Those who have empathy—an Idealist/Blue strength—can see the world through their students' perspective. Sometimes adolescents interpret sympathy as justification for poor performance. Instead of expressing sympathy, teachers need to communicate that they are going to help students solve their own problems. Let's revisit our middle school dancers from this perspective.

Our Guardian/Gold Dancer Hi, it's Tom. Remember me? My teachers like me because I work hard. I pay really close attention to Ms. Toffler when she puts math problems on the board. I like the way she explains things. If I can't figure something out, she gives me clues.

More kids should pay attention to her. I'm not perfect, but at least I keep a notebook with all the clues underlined the way my fifth-grade teacher taught me. If everyone did that, maybe Ms. Toffler would have more time to explain those stupid word problems. I love how she reviews all the key points the day before the test.

I wish there wasn't so much to remember in math. I wish math tests were just about math—you know, numbers, not words. I wish the people that made those state tests wrote the questions the same way Ms. Toffler writes them. My cousin told me that in ninth grade he has to do mostly word problems in math. Man, I don't know what I'm going to do then. I guess I'll just have to work harder.

Our Idealist/Blue Dancer Hi, it's Juan. It's nice to see you again. I'm not doing much better in math at the middle school than I did in elementary. I don't know what happens to me. I

just get a sick feeling in my stomach when I walk through that math door. It's like I can't even think straight. Last night I had this nightmare that I was standing at the smartboard without any clothes on. Everyone was laughing at me, but I couldn't sit down until I finished the problem.

When I looked down at my paper, it was empty. Ms. Toffler put her coat around me so kids wouldn't laugh. But that just made the guys laugh even harder—me in a lady's coat.

I don't know why I'm telling you about my dream. It makes me sound like a dork. My dad says I'm too sensitive anyhow—I need to toughen up. Maybe that's why I'm not good at math. Maybe it's a tough-guy thing. Well, so much for middle school being a new start. I like Ms. Toffler, but she can't do my math for me. Sometimes I just want to disappear.

Our Rational/Green Dancer I'm Lakya. You probably remember me. I'm loving middle school. I'm in all the advanced classes. The other day, one of my old friends from elementary school said that I'm a genius.

I'm not really a genius, and it made me mad when she said that. I don't know why I get school stuff—especially math. I told her that if she watches me at the dance next week (I'll be dancing with an eighth grader, Jared) she'll see I'm no goody-two-shoes, no goofy geek.

I like doing well in school, but some of the boys seem to avoid me. Jamal said he wouldn't want a girlfriend who makes him feel dumb. Maybe that's why I like eighth-grade boys. Well, anyhow, I'm doing great in math so far. My scores are slipping a little bit, but I'm still getting mostly A's, and I don't have to study much at all. I stay after school for math club, but that's because it's the only time I get to be with the eighth graders at school.

Our Artisan/Orange Dancer Hey, Jamal—whoa, is middle school a blast or what? I'm not doing any better in math, but I like Ms. Toffler. She's funny, and she tries to make math interesting. She doesn't care if I get up to sharpen my pencil, and she doesn't let anybody laugh if I answer a question wrong. She says everyone will use the smartboard to show their work, but she doesn't force you as long as she knows you have your homework done. Math is starting to make sense to me now, but I missed a lot of stuff (fractions, decimals, and that kind of stuff) because I moved to so many schools in elementary.

I'm most excited about track. We have a middle school track team, and if I can keep my grades up, the coach says I can probably make varsity. Ms. Toffler said she'll work with me in the math lab. Maybe I can get caught up if I'm willing to work hard enough. Ms. Toffler's really cool. I guess most of the middle school teachers aren't as mean as Mrs. Beck thought they'd be. Maybe she just never met them before.

What does Ms. Toffler have to think *about* before she has her students think *aloud?* According to research by Tom Rath and the Gallup agency (2007), most teachers and parents would say she should focus on addressing students' deficits.

Rath suggests, instead, that adults should focus more on students' *strengths zone,* building on their strengths. He describes these strengths zones as talents or personality traits that remain stable over time. For our purposes, think of strengths as the places on the dance floor where students and teachers feel most comfortable—Guardian/Gold, Idealist/Blue, Rational/Green, and Artisan/Orange. If we know how students process information, we can help them focus their attention on specific skills to improve their thinking. We can teach them to think about their thinking in order to improve it. This is the very definition of critical thinking according to Paul and Elder (2002).

A Math Dance that Leads to Critical Thinking

Ms. Toffler can use critical thinking to build the bridge as she walks on it (Quinn 2004). She can use this bridge between her thinking and her students' thinking to adjust her instructional strategies as she teaches. She can adapt her thinking to meet their needs.

Math and the Middle School Dance

It's important to note that critical thinking requires Ms. Toffler to choreograph a dance that's performed on the Green portion of the dance floor, a place where she doesn't dance a great deal of the time. She's not a master at conducting a think aloud activity. But she's an effective manager and quite capable of following sequential procedures. She can use her empathy as a bridge to critical thinking by practicing a think aloud and reflecting on it with her peers. Ms. Toffler and most of her colleagues will want to practice a think aloud several times before it becomes a regular part of their daily instructional routines. After all, practice makes perfect—right?

Not exactly—Ms. Toffler may assume that once her students can demonstrate the think aloud process, they've become better thinkers. In reality, the only thing she'll know for certain is how well they can mimic her behavior. Tom is a Guardian/Gold. He'll mimic Ms. Toffler but still express a desire to *just do math*. To Tom, that means practicing a series of math exercises limited to a specific math algorithm. Word problems are a threat, because Tom has to make his own decisions about which algorithm(s) to use.

Lakya is a Rational/Green dancer. She'll be bored with the think aloud process. She does that intuitively. Thinking is her strength. Juan is an Idealist/Blue dancer. He'll find the think aloud to be every bit as confusing as trying to maintain a notebook. It will simply be one more thing for him to remember. And Jamal—the Artisan/Orange dancer—will be uncertain which he's supposed to remember. He'll ask, "Which are we doing, the notebook thing or the thinky-do thing?"

In planning for instruction, Ms. Toffler can develop a set of critical questions that require students to justify or explain their answers. She can use these questions to guide her students' thinking. She can base them on Paul and Elder's critical thinking standards (2002). When she becomes more comfortable—able to manage them as a normal part of her instructional routine—she can say to students, "Have you noticed the kinds of questions I've been asking you these past several days/weeks? These are critical thinking questions I use to see where your thinking may be breaking down. I want to help you create your own critical questions so you can manage your learning when I'm not there to help you."

Ms. Toffler's critical questions determine how she'll choreograph the dance in the spaces between the notes. She can use them to help students tackle complex problems involving higher order thinking skills such as analysis, synthesis, and evaluation. Her lessons become less of a recital and more of an inquiry process, a process that begins with understanding how her students process information.

Figure 2.3 illustrates sample questions she can use to extend the think aloud process beyond students explaining what they did to explaining the logic behind what they did.

Figure 2.3
Asking Critical Questions

Clarity:	Could you explain the commutative process in your own words?
Accuracy:	Would your answer be correct for a negative number?
Precision:	Why would an astronaut care how many decimal places you used to calculate his reentry angle?
Relevance:	Which words matter in this problem, and why?
Depth:	Could you solve this problem if we changed the fractions to decimals?
Breadth:	Can you state a principle that applies to all of today's problems?
Logic:	Based on what you've told me, can you explain why you chose to divide in step 3?
Significance:	Can you use the number line to explain why the sign is important in this problem?
Fairness:	Why would the median provide a more complete picture of wealth in this example than would the mean?

"I've been practicing these questions with you so I could become more comfortable using them myself. Now I want you to learn how to ask better questions of me and of one another. This is how I'll help you learn to manage your own thinking.

By learning to be more precise in your questions, you can help me help you."

Teachers engage students in higher order thinking (analysis, synthesis, and evaluation) on a daily basis. But higher order thinking isn't the same thing as critical thinking. The challenge for Ms. Toffler is addressing instruction in terms of a set of standards: helping students bring clarity, accuracy, and precision to their reflections; helping them focus on information that's relevant to their purpose with depth, breadth, and logic; helping them differentiate between significant and insignificant information; and ensuring that they consider multiple problem solving protocols (Paul and Elder 2002). Here are other examples of instructional planning questions Ms. Toffler and her colleagues can ask one another as they practice critical thinking:

1. Have we established an internal rubric that aligns our expectations for students with those expressed in state curriculum standards and Common Core standards (what teaching to the Common Core standards looks like in the classroom)?

2. Have we answered test items ourselves and discussed why certain answers are correct or incorrect?

3. Have we practiced think aloud strategies so we can model them for/with students?

4. Have we discussed tools (think aloud, etc.) that would be appropriate to model for/with students in this area?

5. Will we require students to select and defend appropriate thinking strategies (tools) both in class and on tests?

Preparing for the Next Dance

Does practice make perfect? N*ot exactly*—practicing the right things makes perfect. Students need to do more than answer higher order thinking questions designed by teachers. Those questions help them make links to prior learning, but that's only one aspect of critical thinking. When we teach for critical thinking, we model and expect students to learn how to *think about their thinking.* When students practice critical thinking related to meaningful content, they begin to see patterns in their thinking that help or hinder their achievement of grade level expectations.

For students like Juan and Jamal, we may need to design multiple activities that compensate for attention-span deficits while increasing their ability to extend their attention span. Tom may need support to risk being wrong—going outside the Guardian/Gold lines on the dance floor. We may need to demonstrate to students like Lakya that she needs a way to judge her thinking rather than simply saying, "I don't know how I do it. It just comes naturally."

We need to recognize students' natural talents and give them the tools they need to build those talents into strengths. This requires that we create a classroom environment that accepts mistakes as part of learning. We can communicate that it isn't wrong to make mistakes; it's wrong to allow our mistakes to become an excuse for giving up. When students learn that complex problems may require them to test multiple solutions, they see value in reflecting on mistakes as well as successes. They learn that critical thinking is a necessary aspect of managing their own learning. In the next chapter we'll consider the role of critical thinking in helping students gain the confidence they need to identify and solve complex problems.

I Can Dance

Is Critical Thinking the Key to Success?

Math teachers deal with multiple *chicken or egg* questions on a daily basis. They recognize that Common Core standards require students to think critically. Here are a couple

> *...learning differences are not exactly the same thing as learning deficits.*

examples of seventh grade math standards: 1) *"...to extend their understanding of ratios and proportionality to solve single- and multi-step problems...and 2) "to develop a unified understanding of number, recognizing fractions, decimals (that have a finite or a repeating decimal representation), and percents as different representations of rational numbers..."*

Even adults have to read these standards several times to understand them. Is it any wonder that teachers ask, "What do those Common Core standards look like in the classroom? Is critical thinking the key to success?"

Such questions keep philosophers busy and keep teachers in a constant state of flux, trying to make sense of competing reform movements. In chapter 1, we used temperament to demonstrate that differences are *not exactly* the same thing as deficits. This critical distinction marks the first step toward transforming schools into places that celebrate differences. Once we convince students they were born with special talents, it becomes easier to convince them that they can manage their own learning. It's easier to strengthen talents than to fix deficits.

This doesn't mean we turn students loose to pursue naive interests or that we simply ignore deficits. It means that we teach students to think like entrepreneurs. Entrepreneurs stick with things that pay the greatest return on their investment. Entrepreneurs know how to develop a niche market. That's why we said in chapter 2 that practice doesn't make perfect. Practicing the right things makes perfect. When students practice thinking aloud in class, they have opportunities to compare their thinking with others. This exposes thinking that may be blocking their path to success.

> *Entrepreneurs stick with things that pay the greatest return on investment.*

Figure 3.1
Where Teachers Dance

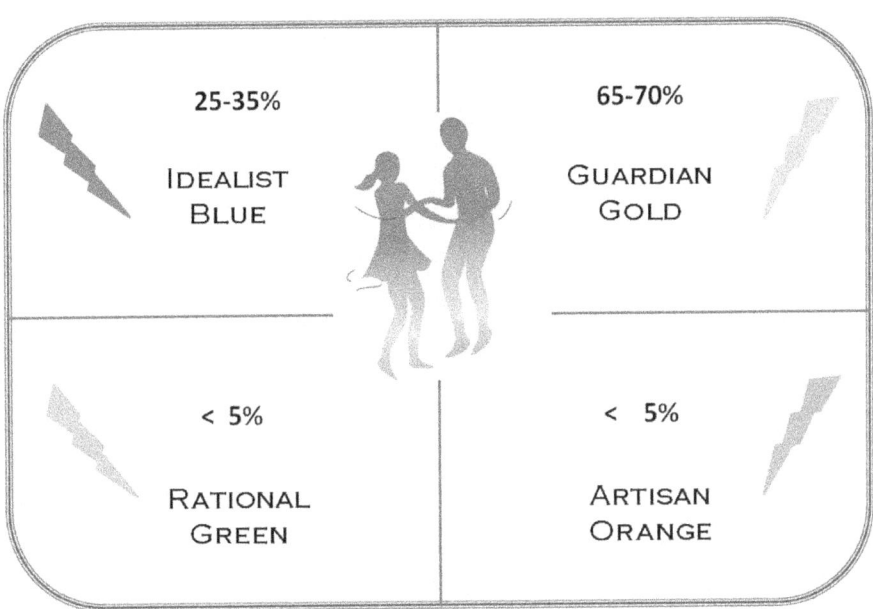

Let's return to the dance floor to consider the question, "Is critical thinking the key to success?" Figure 3.1 may help us answer this question.

This figure illustrates that 65 to 70 percent of teachers spend most of their time on the Guardian/Gold portion of the dance floor (www.keirsey.com). These individuals believe that success comes from hard work and sacrifice. They learn by listening and following directions. Notice also the percentage of teachers who dance on the Idealist/Blue portion of the floor. When the percentages of these Guardian/Gold and Idealist/Blue teachers are added together, they make up approximately 90 percent of the adults in any school.

Is it surprising that schools value rules, order, and service? Should we be surprised that teachers tell adolescents they can be anything they want to be if they work hard enough? Should we be surprised to hear them say, "No one cares how much you know until they know how much you care?" These values around hard work and concern for others aren't a bad thing. They're just *not exactly* the only ingredients for success.

Tom and his Guardian/Gold peers, who learn math the way their teachers teach, sit in the catbird seat. Juan and his Idealist/Blue peers, who value being liked over being right, at least get credit for trying. Both groups try to follow directions. They have a natural inclination for what Covey (1989) calls beginning with the end in mind—tell me what to do, and I'll try my best to do it.

If these students know exactly what teachers expect of them, they can chunk information long enough to remember it for a test. Their success becomes a matter of achieving the teachers' expectations. Chunking concepts and complex problems into manageable pieces provides multiple opportunities for *most* Guardian/Gold and *many* Idealist/Blue students to achieve success in school. But it's *not exactly* the best practice for dealing with real world ambiguities.

Let's consider how the overall temperament of a school (the school culture) stacks the deck for or against various students. Few teachers in any content area are Artisan/Orange. People who dance on the Orange portion of life's dance floor want to interpret the music through unique and original dance moves. They look for excitement wherever they can find it. These

Artisan/Oranges have a difficult time tolerating the daily routines required to manage a classroom.

Likewise, Rational/Greens, who make up less than 10 percent of the general population, are unlikely to be attracted to teaching, especially at the middle school level. Don't forget, middle school students are bouncing around the dance floor trying to figure out where they belong. One moment they're acting like helpless children. The next moment they're gathering like a herd of elk during rutting season. There's no logic to attract Rational/Greens to this environment. They don't fit.

We tend to forget that adults exercise a tremendous level of control over a child's day to day environment. We have the power to add our expertise to the educational process. We even have the power to coerce or cajole students into doing things *our way*. But this doesn't mean that doing things our way in school equates to becoming more successful outside of school. Success in school doesn't necessarily equate to success in life.

Not all children learn to dance by watching someone else dance. Teaching is not a recital. It is a dynamic dance in the spaces between where test scores show learners performing and where the Common Core standards indicate they should be performing. As Quinn (2004) suggests, we have to teach students to "build the bridge as they walk on it."

Guardian/Gold learners approach thinking as a series of building blocks that lead from one success to the next. Idealist/Blue learners approach it as a process of trying to please their teachers. Artisan/Orange learners leap from one solution to the next, oblivious to any connections. And Rational/Green learners try to figure out how to get what they want in as many steps as required but in as few as possible.

Let's be honest. It's easier to work with students who learn the way we teach or with those who at least don't resist our teaching methods. But effective teachers help students build their own bridges to success rather than building the bridges for them. This means guarding against the tendency to over-control classroom learning.

Too much control creates an unrealistic sense of success for middle school students who define learning as doing what they're told. It creates excuses for students who believe they're being coerced into doing what they don't want to do. It ignores the fact that real world events don't always lead directly to a point where someone has already constructed a bridge across the learning abyss. Learning is about building the bridge as we walk on it.

Success Builds Bridges

The most effective way to develop self confidence, or efficacy, comes from reflecting on our own success. Bandura (1977, 1997) calls this a *mastery experience*. Success builds bridges to self efficacy, and self efficacy builds bridges to success. Most of us stick with strategies that work, but self efficacy evolves over years, not over weeks or months. The speed of that evolution is determined as much by the nature of the learner as by the nature of the teacher or the content.

Critical thinking is a necessary element for achieving self efficacy—the ability to manage our own learning. To manage our own learning, we need to reflect on our thinking before, during, and after an event. To achieve mastery in math or any other endeavor, it's important that we not only reflect, but that we also focus those reflections on recognizing patterns.

Students build self efficacy by developing multiple ways to solve problems. They need to know which sequence works best for them and how that sequence impacts the accuracy and time required to arrive at a problem solution. Figure 3.2 presents four sources or strategies for developing self efficacy (Bandura 1977).

Figure 3.2
Sources of Self Efficacy

Mastery experience	achieving success
Social modeling	observing how other people achieve success
Social persuasion	being convinced by others that we have the ability to achieve success
Psychological response	recognizing how moods, emotional states, physical reactions, and stress levels can impact achievement

Most math teachers today don't accept correct answers as proof that students understand mathematical patterns. They expect students to justify their answers. While such reflections are important, it's equally important for students to reflect on the patterns in their thinking that enhance or inhibit their success over time.

This type of reflection requires more than repeating the steps in a prescribed algorithm. Students need to be able to explain why that algorithm was appropriate for the problem at hand. They also need to develop a capacity to justify their thinking according to their own evaluative criteria. This is the essence of self efficacy—to develop an internal evaluation process that allows us to reflect on our thinking as we work toward a problem solution or goal. Remember, middle school brains are only beginning to develop the ability to make these abstract judgments.

The significance of the mastery experience goes beyond ensuring success for students. It requires students to practice making reasoned judgments. They learn how to self monitor by reflecting on the unique conditions that led to their success across multiple learning experiences. Our words and actions should convey a nonjudgmental observation and feedback loop. Otherwise, students will continue to rely on our evaluative criteria rather than developing their own. Such reflections depend as much on the nature of the student as they do on the nature of the content.

> *The challenge for teachers is deciding how to use social modeling, social persuasion, and psychological response strategies to make problem solving less threatening.*

Is Critical Thinking the Key to Success?

Every student needs multiple mastery experiences to develop self efficacy. Unfortunately, as Jonah Lehrer suggests in *Imagine* (2012), success often deters creativity. We never outgrow the danger of pleasing others at the expense of stifling our own creativity. It's natural to follow the path of least resistance. The challenge for teachers is deciding how to use social modeling, social persuasion, and psychological response strategies to make problem solving less threatening.

A Rational/Green like Lakya may need little more than social persuasion from Ms. Toffler to experience mastery.

You know, I've been reflecting on your work. It's obvious you understand the concepts. You never miss the challenge problems. Perhaps you're rushing through the simple problems and making calculation errors. What would you think if I gave you fewer but more complex problems on each assignment?

For an Artisan/Orange like Jamal, she may need to focus on avoiding criticisms that create a battle of wills. Instead of saying, "You just don't pay attention," she might say,

I've noticed that you can solve equations with whole numbers, but you struggle with fractions. Would it help if I gave you two exact equations except that one had only whole numbers and the other had fractions? That way we could make certain you learn the process as we reinforce your fraction skills.

For a Guardian/Gold like Tom, Ms. Toffler may need to take a different approach to stress avoidance.

You know, I've been observing you, and you can solve complex problems when you follow my specific directions. Let's see what happens if I give you a problem that I've already solved and have you tell me what the math concepts and sequences are. This may help you take the emphasis off the right answer and place it on your thinking.

For an Idealist/ Blue like Juan, she may need to suggest a particular thinking tool.

You know, I've been impressed with your ability to see the big picture. You seem to get confused when you have to break things into parts and then put them back together. I think the part to whole thinking map might help you see how the pieces fit together. You could start by writing the question you're being asked to answer and then list the things you know.

Most of us were trained to *do* math rather than to reason mathematically. We were taught to follow directions rather than to think. We were told what we were doing wrong, but we weren't shown how to fix it—other than by paying more attention, working harder, or sitting still. Our math teachers demonstrated mathematical algorithms and had us practice them until we could perform them automatically.

> *Most of us were trained to* do *math rather than how to reason mathematically.*

Is Critical Thinking the Key to Success?

This kind of social modeling didn't require us to think. It required us to mimic our teachers. The emphasis was on *what* we were doing rather than on thinking about *how* we were doing it. It didn't matter whether we felt comfortable or uncomfortable in the process. Learning math in this way was like practicing polka steps only to discover later that the band only knows how to play hip-hop. Right steps, wrong dance floor.

To meet the expectations for math as presented through the Common Core standards, students need to be fully engaged in mathematical reasoning. But engagement doesn't guarantee success. We have to balance personal needs with the needs of those around us. This is what Quinn (2002) calls *authentic engagement.* Sympathy is about helping someone less fortunate. Empathy involves seeing the world through their eyes so we can help them find their own solutions.

Can we see the world of a math classroom through the students' eyes? What do they know? What don't they know? What have they learned but forgotten? Based on their limited years of experience, *what do they not know that they don't know?* Do they have a realistic vision of their innate talents? Have the adults in their lives given them opportunities to apply those talents within multiple contexts—what Quinn refers to as building *adaptive confidence?* Have they learned to explore other sources of information before relying on teachers for

> *Sympathy is about helping someone less fortunate. Empathy involves seeing the world through their eyes so we can help them find their own solutions.*

approval? Do they know that it's all right to stumble as long as they can determine what got in their way?

Teaching strategies need to be grounded in a vision of students' strengths and in a commitment to equipping them with tools that work for them. To engage authentically with students in math and for them to engage authentically with one another, all parties need to acknowledge what they do well and where they struggle.

This acknowledgement begins with the teacher. We can't forget that the chances are seven in ten that a teacher will be a sequential learner. Can we accept that not everyone learns sequentially? Can we accept that some students are so overwhelmed by the fear of being wrong (being made a fool in front of their peers) that they can't focus on our explanations?

Toward Entrepreneurial Thinking

Teachers can help students become entrepreneurial thinkers by helping them develop the confidence to adapt to new situations. We can teach students to compare and contrast current problems with others where they have already achieved success. It's the old *what you know versus what you need to know* strategy. That is, we can help students determine what they're good at, what others are good at, and how they can learn from one another.

Is Critical Thinking the Key to Success?

Analytical thinkers can learn that their best ideas may go unnoticed if they can't explain them in a straightforward, logical sequence. Obedient followers can learn that teachers won't always be there to explain which set of procedures they should follow. At risk and risk-averse students may need smaller sets of problems so they don't feel compelled to rush their thinking to meet time constraints. If students are to improve their thinking, they need to correct misconceptions before they become bad habits.

> *If students are to improve their thinking, they need to correct misconceptions before they become bad habits.*

Entrepreneurial thinking is about engaging with other people without losing sight of our own talents. We depend on feedback from others to grow. We can teach students like Tom and Juan (Guardian/Golds and Idealist/Blues) to use external feedback to develop their own internal feedback loops. Quinn calls this *detached interdependence,* a skill that allows us to work effectively with others without becoming totally dependent on their judgments.

Entrepreneurial thinking also requires what Quinn calls an awareness of *responsible freedom*—identifying the skills and information we need before we embark on a problem solving task. We need to teach students like Lakya and Jamal (Rational/Greens and Artisan/Oranges) that accepting help from someone else isn't a sign of weakness. We can help students develop a balance between internal and external feedback loops by teaching them to ask themselves the Paul and Elder clarifying questions before they turn to someone else for help. These questions help them take responsibility for knowing when and how to seek specific help from others. When they need help, they will be able to state their needs with clarity, depth, and precision.

Perhaps one of the most difficult steps toward helping students build this entrepreneurial bridge as they walk on it is what Quinn calls *tough love*. Tough love requires more than forcing reluctant students to *give it a try*. It requires more than watering down problems or prompting students at every turn of a problem solving situation.

Tough love requires teachers to create an environment in which mistakes become a natural part of the problem solving process. For students like Juan, this may mean allowing them to become *engaged observers* who write down the steps that other students use during a think aloud. These Idealist/Blues can see others struggling through mistakes until they arrive at a correct solution. Then they may be willing to try a problem on their own as others provide feedback. Wilhelm's research (2001) suggests that reluctant learners are more likely to gain a sense of self efficacy by watching another student struggle through the problem rather than watching the teacher. They expect their teachers to know the answers.

The tough part of tough love is often tougher on the teacher than it is on the students. Because seven in ten teachers are driven by time and sequence, it's hard to allow

> *The tough part of tough love is often tougher on the teacher than it is on the students.*

adequate time and support for a struggling Juan, a distracted Jamal, or an argumentative Lakya. That's the love part. Tough love isn't about memorizing the elements of critical thinking (Paul and Elder 2002). It's about using the elements and clarifying questions to establish a classroom environment that encourages and supports entrepreneurial thinking.

Learning to Lead the Entrepreneurial Dance

Students need more than encouragement to help them organize their thinking. They need tools that help them when no one is available to provide encouragement or to think aloud with them. In some situations, such as during a test, thinking aloud could give an unfair advantage or cause confusion for other students. To become responsible managers of their own learning, students need to learn how to dance solo when they don't have a partner. Once students are able to articulate their thoughts in terms of the Paul and Elder critical thinking standards (clarity, accuracy, precision, etc.) they can begin to build their own bridges to self efficacy.

Thinking maps similar to those shown in figure 3.3 (Inspiration Thinking Maps 2010) provide a bridge for students to move from managing concrete problems to managing abstract ideas. As they read a concept description or as they watch a problem solving demonstration, they can complete a thinking map. After students complete that task, volunteers can walk through their maps with the rest of the class. Other students can ask questions that require the presenters to clarify steps or provide more precise explanations.

Figure 3.3
Sample Thinking Maps

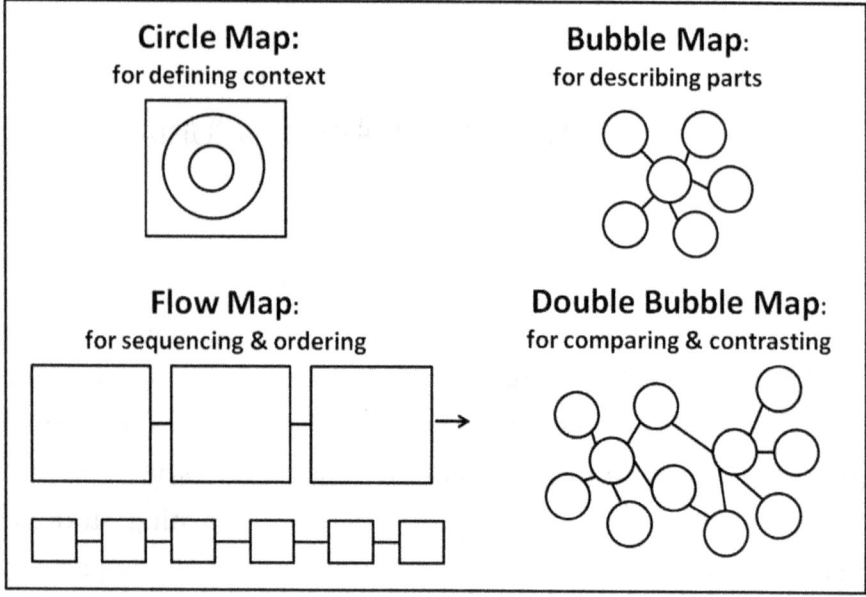

Students might place a mathematical definition—for example, the commutative process of addition—in the center circle of the circle map and then list examples of problems that demonstrate the process in the outer circle. They might use a flow map to illustrate the steps for solving an equation. The top squares indicate the major steps in the process. The smaller squares indicate sub-steps.

Thinking maps illustrate relationships. They show how one idea or process relates to another. Is it an example? Is it a major or a minor step in the process? Or, in the case of the double bubble map, is one concept or process similar to or different from another?

By using thinking tools, students can become more aware of their own thinking processes and see how other people approach a problem differently. If they analyze not only what works but also what doesn't work, they can develop ways to improve their thinking. They can see and hear the thinking behind the answer. They can move from simply practicing math algorithms to practicing mathematical thinking—a significant factor in learning to manage their own learning in terms of the Common Core standards for math.

Entrepreneurs Manage Their Own Success

Self efficacy involves more than thinking about our thinking. It involves making conscious decisions to improve our thinking processes. An idea isn't a strategy, and a strategy isn't a plan. Action plans involve expectations, an awareness of existing skills/performance levels, and an awareness of what learners know and don't know. They involve strategies, timelines, and logistics.

Just as students need tools to improve their critical thinking skills, they need tools to manage their thinking from one problem solving situation to the next. Such tools allow students to improve not only what they're practicing but also how they're practicing. Figure 3.4 provides an example of how teachers can help students focus on improving their entrepreneurial thinking skills.

Figure 3.4
Personal Growth Plan

Name _____ Unit _____

Year _____ 9 Weeks _____

Expected performance level:

My current performance level:

My problem solving strengths:

Goals:

Improve my ability to:

_____ Identify the question to be answered

_____ Distinguish between important and unimportant information

_____ Recognize faulty assumptions

_____ Draw comparisons and contrasts

_____ Follow a sequence

_____ Recognize part to whole relationships

_____ State my ideas/questions with more clarity/precision/and depth

_____ Be careful with computations

_____ See patterns in my mistakes so I can correct them

_____ Other _____

My specific plan is to (write 1-3 sentences describing practice times, places, and timelines):

I will work with _____ to get feedback on my progress because he/she/they are good at:

I will share my progress with my teacher _____ times per week.

Entrepreneurs often aren't experts in any one thing, but they're not afraid to make mistakes. They simply recognize that problem solving requires them to manage the risks involved. They know their success depends on more than correct information. It requires planning, good timing, and an ability to know when they need to find a dance partner.

Keep on Dancing

Critical thinking is *not exactly* the key to success. Entrepreneurs also have a strong sense of self efficacy. They aren't afraid to act on hunches. They accept mistakes as part of the learning process. They're willing to fill in the blanks as they go.

In the past two chapters, we've considered the question of *what* to manage (critical thinking and self efficacy). The question that arises for many teachers at this point is, "When can I find time to manage thinking and goal setting with everything else I have to do? I have to create and score homework and tests. I have to record grades and plan lessons. Given the range of differences in my students' performance, I frequently have to create intervention and extension activities to differentiate my instruction."

In part 2 we'll consider *how* we can use digital technology to manage many of these instructional routines. We'll also consider the tasks it's realistic for us to expect computers to perform. Then we'll consider the most difficult problem of all: changing instructional habits that prevent us from taking full advantage of digital technology to teach entrepreneurial thinking. In the final chapter, we'll consider how the nature of what we evaluate determines the extent to which our schools promote and sustain an entrepreneurial culture.

Part II

Mastering the Digital Two-Step:

Managing an Entrepreneurial Culture

PART II

Reach Back–Teach Forward

Are Thinking Skills more Important than Content?

Many of today's careers didn't exist ten years ago, and many won't exist ten years from now. This means we'll see not only an increase in information, but an increase in the speed at which information becomes obsolete. From digital tablets and laptops to super colliders, we have the means to model events in ways that decrease the risks involved in entrepreneurial ventures. This computer modeling capability doesn't negate the importance of content; it redefines the skills needed to deal with content in innovative ways.

Mathematics played a significant role in growing the US economy during the 20th Century. Entrepreneurs used formulas to make decisions that increased business and manufacturing efficiencies.

> *Entrepreneurs in a digital world need to know more than math processes; they need to process ideas and information mathematically.*

Scientists used math to calculate and navigate the distance to heavenly bodies. Using computer modeling, we can now simulate and manipulate the impacts of change from the molecular level to the deepest reaches of space. The role of technology in this modeling process doesn't decrease the importance of math content; it changes the way we use math in our daily lives.

Thinking skills aren't *exactly* more important than content. They go hand in hand. Entrepreneurs in a digital world need to know more than math processes; they need to process ideas and information mathematically. They need to think about their thinking in terms of new and existing math models.

The remainder of this book focuses on the critical relationship between thinking skills and content. We'll consider how teachers can manage this relationship to create as many mastery experiences as possible in their classrooms. Finally, we'll consider how principals and central office administrators can manage schools to produce a marketable intellectual product—entrepreneurial thinkers. We begin by considering how teachers like Ms. Toffler can use digital technology to manage instructional routines and maximize entrepreneurial thinking in her classroom.

Students like Tom, Lakya, Juan, and Jamal learn differently. Instead of celebrating and encouraging these differences as sources of creative thinking, we treat them as deficits to be repaired. We assume they all need to march along a similar path to arrive at a problem solution. This assumption limits differentiation to matters of memory and pacing. It also affects how we view the role of technology in improving math instruction.

When it comes to digital technology, Mr. Chang recognizes that access to the right equipment is only part of the problem. Let's reexamine Mr. Chang's earlier words.

Thanks to the superintendent's commitment to technology, my school will still receive the computers, software, and other digital equipment we were promised last spring. But I'll have to convince the staff to attend after school professional development, with little or no chance of pay, so they can learn how to use the new software and equipment.

My teachers know that computers have replaced pencils and paper, interactive electronic boards have replaced chalkboards and whiteboards, and Internet videos have replaced filmstrips and movies. But much more change will be required.

The change Mr. Chang is referring to runs counter to the assumptions driving today's classrooms. For example, take a look at the table of contents in any math textbook. Notice that the first several chapters focus on a review of concepts from previous grades. The challenging aspects of math appear at the end of the book—the area Ms. Toffler and her students won't have time to reach.

For more than a decade, we've known that US math teachers spend nine weeks or more each year reviewing previously taught concepts (TIMSS 1995-2011). This leaves the core of the curriculum—the grade level expectations—to be taught during the remaining 75 percent of the school year. Now add two to three weeks to prepare for state testing each spring and another week for the testing itself. This means students are spending as much as one-third of the school year on testing and review activities.

It shouldn't surprise anyone that Ms. Toffler has to sacrifice depth for efficiency. It shouldn't surprise anyone that, in her haste to cover the content, Ms. Toffler might confuse a tricky word problem with one that requires complex mathematical reasoning. Placing simple math routines inside a confusing array of word problems is *not exactly* the same thing as creating mathematical complexity. Confusing students with tricky words is, at best, a test of their reading skills.

Even if Ms. Toffler doesn't follow the table of contents as a lockstep march, is it realistic to assume she can adequately address grade level math expectations given the wide array of needs among her students? According to the TIMSS research, it isn't. So, let's consider how we can use digital technology to turn this march to nowhere into an entrepreneurial dance.

Digitizing the Dance

Most math software is designed to manage content, assessment, and practice routines. This design connects Ms. Toffler's grade book, textbook, and workbook, but it doesn't address her tier 1 instructional planning. (*Tier1* instruction simply means the instruction Ms. Toffler routinely provides for all students on a daily basis.) Today's software accelerates existing instructional routines without necessarily improving them.

Over the past five years, I've worked with an economics expert, Dr. Woo Jung, who has been field testing an online math program he developed specifically to improve tier 1 math instruction. As a math practitioner who struggled with math in school, Dr. Jung believes math instruction can be more than a logical sequential march involving memorization and mimicry.

> *Today's software accelerates existing instructional routines without necessarily improving them.*

Dr. Jung's software, T-S Nexus, was originally developed for use in South Korea. It was the only online program created by a private company to be approved by the Korean Institute for Curriculum and Evaluation (2003) for use in South Korean schools. It was when Dr. Jung began to redesign T-S Nexus to meet the National Council of Teachers of Mathematics (NCTM) standards in the US that he saw a way to combine the South Korean focus on mathematical reasoning with the US focus on innovative thinking.

Field tests of T-S Nexus in more than 25 US schools in 5 states indicate gains in test scores as high as 40 percent. The average increase of students performing at proficient or advanced levels on state tests is 18 percent. Equipment needs are minimal.

1. Computers (or netbooks) with Internet connection

2. Classroom or lab computer access for students two times per week for approximately thirty to forty-five minutes

3. Daily teacher access to a computer and a projector

Figure 4.1 illustrates the T-S Nexus table of contents for seventh grade.

Figure 4.1
A Digital Table of Contents

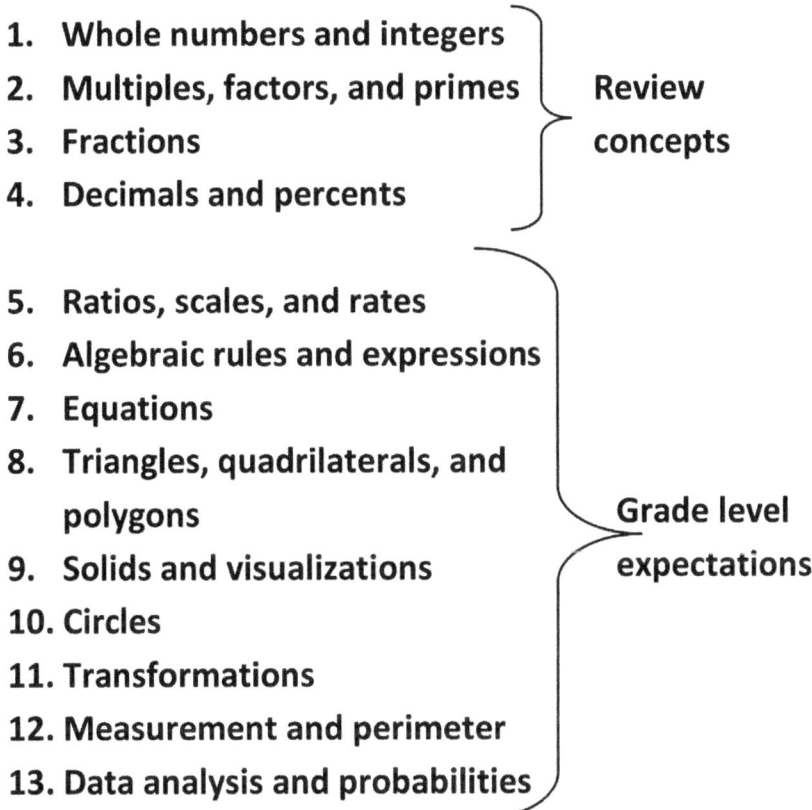

This table of contents looks like any textbook table—organized in a logical sequential manner for management purposes. However, the digital links within T-S Nexus allow teachers the flexibility to make assignments from several chapters or even from another grade level. Unlike other software programs, T-S Nexus is not limited to a logical sequential march. It links adaptive individualized assignments to teacher created customized assignments and tests. It links textbook examples and concept summaries to each of more than 50,000 problems.

Perhaps the most significant feature of T-S Nexus is how it links error analysis directly to tier 1 classroom instruction. Like most digital programs, it provides various analytical tables and reports. But it also identifies problems that most students struggled with on an assignment and allows teachers to save them for follow up lessons. Rather than taking the time for students to write problem solutions (correct or incorrect) on the board, Ms. Toffler can quickly project problems with correct solutions and engage students in a think aloud. As students focus on their own solutions, she can encourage them to ask questions and identify the obvious (and not so obvious) factors that caused them to arrive at an incorrect answer to the problem.

As a follow up to her classroom instruction, Ms. Toffler can differentiate assignments for various groups of students. Following a pretest and an introductory lesson, for example, Ms. Toffler can provide individualized practice assignments for Guardian/Gold students like Tom and Rational/Green students like Lakya. Individualized assignments within T-S Nexus are adaptive: they adjust the level of difficulty and complexity each time a student completes three problems.

For those Idealist/Blue students like Juan and Artisan/Orange students like Jamal, Ms. Toffler can create shorter customized assignments focused on a more limited set of review skills. T-S Nexus allows Ms. Toffler to control the complexity of problems to review skills from earlier units or previous grade levels. Then the following day she can incorporate past skills into current grade level expectations.

Digital technology can't replace good teachers, but it can improve teachers' productivity. It can help teachers and students manage content and assessment routines. It can become a part of an ongoing feedback loop that incorporates review skills within the context of grade level expectations. Imagine how much time Ms. Toffler and her students could devote to critical thinking and self efficacy if they had access to digital software that managed the following routine functions:

1. Creating tests, quizzes, and individualized homework assignments

2. Scoring, analyzing, and providing error analysis reports for all assignments

3. Providing 24/7 access to assignments and results for students, teachers, parents, and administrators

4. Organizing user friendly information for professional learning communities and data teams

Digital technology doesn't replace content or eliminate the need for direct instruction. It simply allows teachers to differentiate instruction to achieve the greatest positive impact on student performance. Demonstration and practice help students recall facts and procedures, chunk information for use in their active working memory, and categorize information in terms of patterns. However, to retain that information over time and to apply it across multiple situations, students need to develop a deeper understanding of the relationships between and among the embedded mathematical concepts.

To understand how this process develops, it might be helpful to consider what Levine (2002) identifies as the five neurological functions beyond memory that determine how much information Ms. Toffler's students are likely to retain over time. It is in addressing the complexity of these neurological functions that thinking and digital technology meet. Figure 4.2 illustrates several neurological functions involved in mathematical thinking.

Figure 4.2

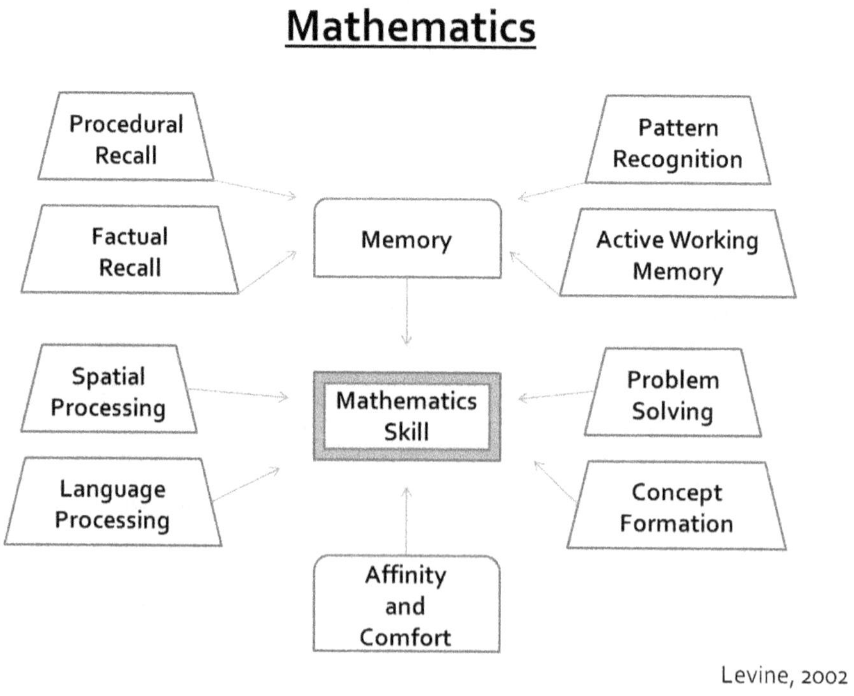

Mathematics

- Procedural Recall
- Factual Recall
- Spatial Processing
- Language Processing
- Memory
- Mathematics Skill
- Affinity and Comfort
- Pattern Recognition
- Active Working Memory
- Problem Solving
- Concept Formation

Levine, 2002

Mathematical reasoning requires problem solving, concept formation, spatial and language processing, and forming an affinity for math. The significance of these factors involves more than their individual impact on learning. It involves the complex interrelationships among the student, the teacher, and the content.

In math classrooms, teachers have to focus on more than the content or the students' thinking. They have to consider how their instructional strategies impact both content and thinking. Figure 4.3 illustrates this point.

Figure 4.3
Colliding Cultures

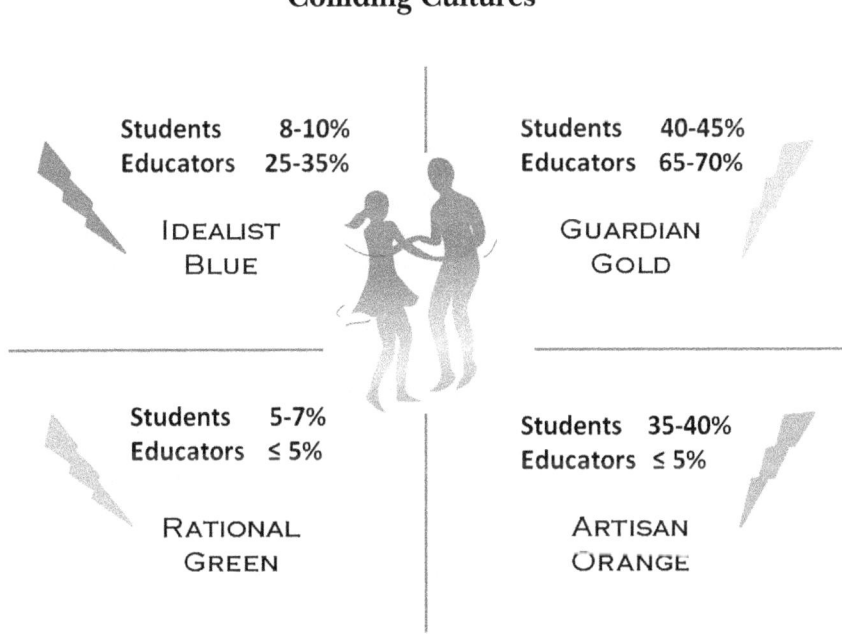

Notice that 65 to 70 percent of teachers are Guardian/Gold processors. Their teaching matches 45 to 50 percent of the students in their classrooms—the Guardian/Gold students like Tom who follows his teachers' expectations. When you combine the staff's Guardian/Gold and Idealist/Blue percentages, you can see that there's almost a 90 percent probability in any school environment that hard work (Guardian) and compliance (Idealist) behaviors will trump logic (Rational) and risk-taking (Artisan) behaviors. Hard work trumps sound logic; correct answers trump creative problem solving; and that which is kind and fair trumps truth and integrity.

If all her students could dance comfortably on any portion of the math dance floor, Ms. Toffler could walk them through a logical sequential lesson with little regard for differentiation. But we've seen that students' brains simply don't process information in exactly the same order or at exactly the same pace. Some students have more difficulty than others when it comes to language processing. Remember Tom's concerns?

> I wish math tests were just about math—you know numbers, not words. I wish the people that made those state tests wrote the questions the same way Ms. Toffler writes them.

Guardian/Gold teachers organize content and instruction into a defined sequence. This allows Guardian/Gold students to meet cultural expectations and Idealist/Blue students to know what they have to do to please their teachers. Artisan/Orange students, on the other hand, are always on the prowl for shortcuts. If they can get to the destination faster, they'll have more time to explore other interests. Rational/Green students are influenced more by what seems logical than by what the teacher expects.

Success in math is determined by more than DNA. It's impacted by students' past experiences and their interest in the content. Forcing Juan, Lakya, and Jamal to function like Tom is like forcing left handed people to write with their right hand. It can be done, but it further complicates an already complex set of neurological functions that determine how students approach a task. Ms. Toffler can use digital tools to help her students fill in experiential gaps and correct their mathematical misconceptions. Let's consider how she can do this using what I call the *digital two-step*.

THE DIGITAL TWO-STEP

I refer to *reaching back* and *teaching forward* as the digital two-step. The only thing new in this classroom management strategy is that digital technology makes it easier. Instead of managing materials and monitoring progress for a wide array of student levels, teachers use technology to integrate remediation and extension activities within their daily (tier 1) classroom instruction. The fundamental premise of *reach back—teach forward* is that teachers don't have time to reteach skills and algorithms that students have already been expected to master. A second, and equally significant point, is that students see remediation as a defeat. No matter what we say, struggling students see themselves as dumb.

Imagine for a moment that Ms. Toffler has a digital math program designed to generate a pretest of the requisite skills for her grade level. Imagine that it immediately reports results in terms of the skills her students did or did not master in previous grades. There's nothing new there, right?

But what if embedded in each assignment (or even each problem) there was a concept review? And what if Ms. Toffler could link that concept review to an error analysis of the specific problems her students encounter in daily assignments? What if the system allowed her to link those problems with similar prototype problems and project them for a small group or for the entire class?

Ms. Toffler would save class time by not having to correct homework assignments in class. She would save more time because students would not have to write problem solutions on the board. She would not have to think up a sample problem to solve or to have students solve for reinforcement. But the advantages of this approach go beyond time savings.

Since the program tells Ms. Toffler who missed which problems, she doesn't need to have incorrect solutions on the board. Jamal has problems limiting his attention and making connections among concepts. He doesn't need to see what Juan did wrong. He needs to see the correct solution and explain where his thinking broke down.

Juan spends most of his time trying to avoid eye contact with Ms. Toffler, hoping she won't call on him. With the correct solution in front of him, he has one less issue to worry about. He'll also see that Tom and Lakya, the students who probably arrived at the correct answer, sometimes have as much trouble as Juan has explaining their thinking. And if Ms. Toffler has a remote control for her computer, she can move freely around the room to refocus students who may be distracted.

Then, as if time savings and a focus on critical thinking weren't enough of a digital benefit, there is the matter of the self efficacy advantage. Ms. Toffler isn't going to let any student off the hook with a simple, "I don't know." To that, she'll reply, "Well, then take a look at the concept review and tell us what you don't understand." Or she might say, "Show us the step you missed, and explain where your thinking went wrong."

This type of instruction facilitates her classroom think aloud. Instead of focusing on who got which answer correct, everyone is focusing on mathematical thinking. By helping students explain and clarify their thinking, Ms. Toffler is communicating, by example, that her students have the ability to solve complex math problems. If they understand the concept, they don't have to mimic her steps.

From any test or assignment, Ms. Toffler can generate two types of follow-up practice assignments? The first would adjust the difficulty and complexity of problems automatically so students like Tom and Lakya could move *forward* at their own pace. The second would customize assignments for students like Juan and Jamal who might need to *reach back* to sharpen skills required to meet grade level expectations. So everything is copacetic, right?

Not exactly—despite all these advantages that we say we would welcome, my experience in numerous digital field tests over the past several years suggests that Ms. Toffler's temperament will interfere with her desire to improve her teaching. Teachers and administrators have become so *schooled* in using technology to manage content, assessment, and record keeping that they have a problem thinking of it as a tier 1 instructional tool. "Come on," they say, "Do you really believe I can work this in with everything else I'm doing?"

> *Teachers and administrators have become so "schooled" in using technology to manage content, assessment, and record keeping that they can't adjust their thinking to use it as a tier 1 tool.*

The answer is, of course not. Ms. Toffler will have to work as hard at letting go of old habits as she does at developing new habits. Her natural tendency will be to group students in terms of those who mastered the content and those who did not. She'll expect students to use software programs to work independently on either remedial or enrichment assignments. That approach undervalues the role of teaching and underestimates the potential of digital technology.

Digital technology can provide a bridge to help Ms. Toffler do what she does best—manage. Mr. Chang doesn't need to teach Ms. Toffler how to manage. He has to help her focus her Guardian/Gold management talents toward enhancing her students' critical thinking and sense of self efficacy. This is the bridge that crosses thinking deficits—we *reach back (with the help of digital technology)* for specific missing skills or content and *teach forward* by incorporating those requisite skills into current grade level expectations.

Using computer generated pretests and error analysis results, Ms. Toffler can differentiate her instruction. She can use the program to create assignments for three groups of students, but she'll need to form the groups according to their strengths rather than deficits.

The first of these three groups, the largest, consists of students whose pretest scores indicate that they're performing at or near grade level. These will primarily be the Rational/Green and Guardian/Gold students like Lakya and Tom. *The second and third* groups consist of students whose pretest results indicate they're performing below level. While both these struggling groups can receive the same assignment, one will consist of the Artisan/Orange Jamals and the other will consist of the Idealist/Blue Juans. It's important to separate the Idealist/Blues and Artisan/Oranges, because the strategies needed to help one group might be confusing or counterproductive for working with the other group.

Ms. Toffler's weekly schedule looks like this:

- one day of reflection on pretest results, with the class using the system generated error analysis and prototype problems (includes individual and class goal setting)

- one to two days of differentiated assignments (system generated assignments in a lab setting)

- - reach back strategies for integrating requisite skills for those who didn't experience mastery on the pretest

  - teach forward strategies for those who have at least demonstrated readiness

- homework assignments directed toward correcting misunderstandings and extending challenges

- one to two days of whole class instruction focused on the grade level expectations (with or without computers)

For struggling students, *reach back* activities involve a review of requisite skills. They may need to review skills taught in a previous unit or at earlier grade levels. But on the whole class instruction days, they'll relate these skills directly to grade level expectations. Ms. Toffler can use digital software to organize and project problems, use paper and pencil, and/or use various hands on strategies.

> *Practicing mathematical algorithms improves test scores. Practicing mathematical reasoning empowers students to take more responsibility for their own learning.*

Practicing mathematical algorithms improves test scores. Practicing mathematical reasoning empowers students to take more responsibility for their own learning. When Ms. Toffler *reaches back* but *teaches forward,* she helps students see the significance of the missing skills within the context of grade level expectations. A more detailed description of *reaching back and teaching forward* appears in figure 4.4. This chart isn't a prescription. It merely illustrates how Ms. Toffler or any other teacher can employ a user-friendly suite of math software tools to manage a classroom focused on critical thinking and self efficacy.

Figure 4.4
Sample Reach Back—Teach Forward Logistics

Day	Technology Tool	Teacher focus	Student Focus
Monday	To project concept summaries and demonstration problems and for students to complete pretest	Concept summaries and prototype problems to explain grade-level concepts. Work through problem solutions with the class.	*Establish Learning Focus* 1. What do I need to be able to do to demonstrate proficiency? 2. How does this relate to what I already know?
Tuesday	To present, score, and analyze a grade-level core assignment	System generated reports summarize performance and set individual and class growth goals.	*Practice Mathematical Reasoning And Set Goals* 1. What was I expected to know? 2. How well did I do? 3. Where did my thinking break down? 4. What do I need to practice to fill in the gaps?
Wednesday	To project problems and solutions (problems answered incorrectly by 30-70% of students on previous day's assignment)	Model "think-aloud" process with a sample problem. Ask clarifying questions as students "think-aloud" through problem solutions. Assign a new set of problems (5-10) for the following day.	*Draw On Others' Thinking* 1. Answer teacher questions: clarity, depth, etc. 2. Ask questions for clarity, depth, etc.
Thursday	To differentiate assignments related to requisite skills completed, scored, and reported	Teacher monitors and works with individuals and groups (Great time for individual or small group conferencing.)	*Review Requisite Skills That Impede My Success In This Unit*
Friday	To project problem solutions	Groups take one problem and agree on a set of problem solving steps. Groups explain solutions and justify each step based on prior knowledge.	*Practice Problem Solving Protocols With Justification*

Because review skills are linked each week to grade level core standards, Ms. Toffler has more class time to focus on critical thinking and narrowing the gap between what is tested and what is retained over time. This *reach back—teach forward* strategy can save twenty or more days of instructional time each year compared to the traditional approach of instruction that isolates review time to the first quarter and requires students to remember those skills throughout the year.

Students who are performing more than one grade below level may require additional intervention time outside the regular classroom. But with the right digital technology, Ms. Toffler can coordinate these intervention classes with regular classroom activities. Students performing at grade level won't need to *reach back* as often or as far as struggling students. Students performing above grade level can be assigned problems that stretch their thinking—*teaching forward*. The right digital technology can help teachers manage content and assessment, leaving more time to monitor students' thinking and adjust instructional strategies accordingly.

Effective math teachers have always tried to engage students in mathematical reasoning. But imagine how much more time could be devoted to this reasoning process if teachers could rely on a suite of technology tools to create, score, analyze, and record assignments. Imagine how much easier it would be to manage the classroom logistics necessary for differentiation. Imagine managing intervention strategies by projecting concept summaries and actual problems that 30 to 70 percent of the students missed from a previous assignment. Imagine students assuming more responsibility for their own learning by engaging in personal goal setting.

BEYOND THE DIGITAL TWO-STEP

Thinking isn't *exactly* more important than content. As educators, we're accustomed to managing content and assessment. We're accustomed to managing input and output. The challenge lies in shifting the focus from managing behaviors to managing what drives those behaviors—critical thinking and self efficacy. That challenge is as much about letting go of old management habits as it is about learning new habits.

In the next chapter, we'll consider how Ms. Toffler or any math teacher can work with colleagues to develop and sustain high-quality *reach back—teach forward* habits. This requires planning for each critical exchange with the same depth that we now apply toward managing content and instruction.

Choreographing the Dance

Don't All Good Teachers Teach Critical Thinking?

The middle school dance floor becomes much more manageable when Ms. Toffler understands how her students think and has the tools to help them improve their thinking. But Ms. Toffler still faces the struggle of letting go of old instructional habits. As we saw in the last chapter, the instructional dance consists of a partnership between teachers and learners. Ms. Toffler has to use her Guardian/Gold talents to manage the Common

Math and the Middle School Dance

Core standards for four different types of learners: Idealist/Blue, Guardian/Gold, Rational/Green, and Artisan/Orange.

Initially, Ms. Toffler leads the math dance. However, her goal is to choreograph it so students can begin to take the lead. Her instructional strategies have to support the development of those new brain cells that impact her student's ability to make sound judgments. This lead change becomes more complex as her students move from the concrete world of elementary school toward the more abstract world of high school and beyond. It requires Ms. Toffler to begin a gradual release of responsibility for critical thinking in direct proportion to students' ability to organize, manage, and assume the risks for their own learning.

Again, tough love is as tough on teachers as it is on students. Remember, Ms. Toffler's dance floor extends beyond the school day.

Really, I love my job. But I also love being a mom. And I'm trying to get my life back together after a difficult divorce. Each day I have to get Ellie off to school. She is a gem, handling the divorce really well, according to her counselor.

After school is sometimes a bit of a problem. I have department meetings and professional learning community sessions. And some nights my teammate and I need to talk about students or plan a unit together. The Skype camera my parents bought me should eliminate one meeting by letting me plan with my partner after Ellie goes to bed.

The complexity of Ms. Toffler's life outside school adds to the complexity of her life in the classroom. Is it surprising that she relies on certain routines to manage her day? Is it surprising that our education system focuses more on learning what to think than how to think? Even the 30 percent of teachers who aren't Guardian/Golds need routines to navigate their way across the middle school dance floor.

Cashman (2008) suggests that it's easier to manage information about things than to understand the nature of things. It's easier to manage achievement than to manage thinking. After all, students can be anything they want to be if they just try hard enough, right?

Hard work and practice don't change how students learn. Hard work and practice won't change how teachers teach. *Self efficacy is about students and teachers recognizing their strengths and liabilities for what they are and dealing with them.* The ability to think about our goals and directions (to think about our thinking) is what sets human beings apart from other species. It's what allows us to work effectively with others to solve real problems.

Planning as Thinking Critically about Content

Content and instruction are no less important to Blue, Green, and Orange learners than they are to Gold learners. The question is, "How do we transform our schools from places that teach students to march to our drumbeat into places that create and support entrepreneurial thinkers?" Figure 5.1 suggests how we might begin this transformation.

Figure 5.1

> Gradual Release for Building Self efficacy
>
> 1. Students assuming the think aloud problem solving role as other students observe (observe thinking)
> 2. Students feeling free to share their problem solving strengths and liabilities openly and specifically related to unit expectations
> 3. The teacher and classmates applying their strengths to improve thinking by asking clarifying questions (Paul and Elder)
> 4. Students working in groups to apply skills they've learned from one another in a teacher guided, collaborative process
> 5. Students completing a personal growth plan explaining when and how they know to ask for outside help and how to incorporate such help into their own problem solving strategies

Most students and teachers achieve some degree of higher order thinking and self efficacy in school. But they don't necessarily focus on how to manage these processes. Individuals who can learn to manage their inherent ability to think at higher levels, to think about their thinking, can improve their chances of becoming entrepreneurial thinkers. It's important to recognize that this level of mastery experience is as illusive to teachers as it is to students. Teachers like Ms. Toffler need to build the bridge to critical thinking and self efficacy as they walk on it (Quinn 2004).

Ms. Toffler can't control her students' thinking. Nor does she need more training on how to fix their thinking. She needs to understand how her habits and beliefs impact her instruction and how that instruction impacts her students' thinking. She has the innate talent to manage learning if we can help her see what critical thinking and self efficacy look like in the classroom.

A consultant can show her what or how to teach. An administrator can observe her classroom to measure her performance against student outcomes. But ultimately Ms. Toffler needs to engage in a process of reflection that shapes her choice of content and instructional strategies. If she creates an instructional product that her students value and employ, she can help them develop their own intellectual marketability.

Without adequate mastery experiences, students and teachers naturally fall back into their individual comfort zones. Change focuses on correcting bad habits. Transformation focuses on building natural talents into intellectual strengths.

> *Can you tell me what critical thinking looks like in the classroom?*

One way to encourage critical thinking about instruction is for teachers to engage with colleagues in an ongoing critical dialogue. This dialogue doesn't begin with the traditional analysis of what students need to know and be able to do in math. It begins with trying to see learning expectations from their students' point of view. This dialogue involves empathy—an Idealist/Blue skill. As we plan for critical thinking and self efficacy, we ask, "Can you tell me what critical thinking looks like in the classroom?" And that question leads to other clarifying questions:

- What are my students doing?

    o What questions will Tom ask?

    o What kinds of problems will overwhelm Juan?

    o How will the students benefit from working individually, in groups, etc.?

    o How will I help students like Jamal maintain focus long enough to achieve a mastery experience?

- What am I doing?

    o What questions will I ask Lakya to challenge her thinking?

    o What kinds of problems will encourage Tom to take more risks and Jamal to take fewer risks at a time?

- o How will I need to organize materials to manage individual, group, and whole-class activities so Juan isn't too overwhelmed to think critically?

- o How will I generate data on student performance and use it to make decisions about acceleration or reteaching?

These questions create authentic engagement between teachers and students rather than promoting the teachers' way of thinking. They provide the criteria for making better judgments—judgments focused on what works rather than on what *should* work. Let's take a closer look at what this kind of planning involves.

Planning with Empathy

Students learn in different ways. Teachers teach in different ways. It isn't easy to change how our brains are wired. But as Jill Bolte Taylor reports in her book, *My Stroke of Insight* (2006) our brains can adapt to different types of thinking. Following a severe stroke, Taylor, a Rational/Green neuroscientist, trained her brain to reprocess information on other parts of the learning dance floor. Remember Tom Rath's concept of finding strengths (2007). Our temperament is programmed into our DNA, but our temperament isn't an excuse for accepting failure. Our strengths are determined by how effectively we balance our own needs with the needs of those around us.

Entrepreneurs don't excel at everything. Idealist/Blues excel at employing empathy to identify and appreciate multiple points of view. Guardian/Golds excel at defining management parameters. Rational/Greens hold to a clearly defined set of principles. Artisan/Oranges are willing to risk setbacks to test potential solutions.

The problem is that most of us know what we know, but few of us understand what we don't know. In *The Social Animal* (2011), David Brookes states it this way, "It is a law of human nature that the more [people] concentrate in one happy pack, the more each of them will come to resemble Donald Trump... By the law of compound egotism, they create this self-reinforcing vortex of smugness, which brings out the most-pleased-with-themselves aspects of their own personalities."

Efficacy is about recognizing how what we don't know impacts what we think we know (our assumptions) about ourselves and others. It

> *Our temperament is programmed into our DNA. Our strengths are determined by how effectively we balance our own needs with the needs of those around us.*

requires a safe environment where we can discuss our assumptions in an open, nonjudgmental, nonpunitive manner.

By now it should be obvious that to sustain new thinking practices, we have to change our instructional practices. But have we considered that in order to change instructional practices, we have to change the way we plan for instruction?

Don't All Good Teachers Teach Critical Thinking?

Planning time has traditionally been about creating assignments, correcting papers, gathering relevant materials, and contacting parents. How would the dynamics of planning time be different if we managed many of those tasks digitally? There would be no less work, but we could manage that work toward different ends.

High achievement isn't a matter of thinking versus content. It isn't a matter of student direction versus teacher direction. What Ms. Toffler and other math teachers accomplish is a direct function of their focus. We need to capture the Idealist/Blue strength of empathy to focus our planning on distinguishing between how we think and how our students think.

> *Chance meetings in the hallway or using Skype after school are no substitute for regularly scheduled meetings with a planned agenda.*

Adolescence is one of the most significant, life changing experiences any individual will ever encounter. Middle school students like Tom, Lakya, Juan, and Jamal are transitioning from dependence to independence. Their lack of experience is both a blessing and a curse. Their transformation toward self efficacy requires both content knowledge and critical thinking. It also requires an ability to manage risks.

So, if critical thinking doesn't replace the need for managing content and instruction, how does it reshape them? Critical thinking requires content to think about—especially for adolescents, whose life experiences are relatively limited. Teaching and learning for these adolescent years require collaboration and teamwork between and among teachers, between teachers and students, and among students themselves.

We often hear, "Oh, we talk with each other daily in the faculty room, in the hallways, and anywhere we get a chance." The problem is that collaborative planning is too important to be left to chance. Chance meetings in the hallway or using Skype after school are no substitute for regularly scheduled meetings with a planned agenda.

Meaningful collaboration requires teachers to share their expertise and their enthusiasm and to weigh critical feedback in terms of their personal talents. It requires them to challenge one another's personal biases and experiential limitations without judging them. It requires a sense of teaming and shared responsibility that goes beyond two or three people chatting in the hallway or the lunchroom. Likewise, it requires more than a semester or a quarterly conversation with students to ensure that they're setting their own realistic learning goals, monitoring their performance, and adjusting their strategies and daily action plans.

Planning for Excellence

In *Be Excellent at Anything* (2011), Tony Schwartz suggests ten enduring principles we can use to make decisions that reflect the openness, integrity, and authenticity required to achieve excellence. Imagine these principles as a poster in every classroom and meeting room in your school. Imagine them at the core of

Don't All Good Teachers Teach Critical Thinking?

every professional conversation among teachers. Notice how they incorporate both Paul and Elder's elements of critical thinking and Bandura's sources of self efficacy.

1. Always challenge certainty, especially your own. When you think you're undeniably right, ask yourself, "What might I be missing here?" If we could truly figure it all out, what else would there be left to do?

2. Excellence is an unrelenting struggle, but it's also the surest route to enduring satisfaction. Amy Chua, the over-the-top Tiger Mother, was right that there's no shortcut to excellence. Getting there requires practicing deliberately, delaying gratification, and forever challenging your current comfort zone.

3. Emotions are contagious, so it pays to know what you're feeling. Think of the best boss you ever had. How did he or she make you feel? That's the way you want to make others feel.

4. When in doubt, ask yourself, "How would I behave here at my best?" We know instinctively what it means to do the right thing, even when we're inclined to do the opposite. In a challenging moment, if you find it impossible to envision how you'd behave at your best, try imagining how someone you admire would respond.

5. If you do what you love, the money may or may not follow, but you'll love what you do. It's magical thinking to

assume you'll be rewarded with riches for following your heart. What it will give you is a richer life. If material riches don't follow, and you decide they're important, there's always time for plan B.

6. You need less than you think you do. All your life, you've been led to believe that more is better and that whatever you have isn't enough. It's a prescription for disappointment. Instead, ask yourself this: How much of what you already have truly adds value to your life? What could you do without?

7. Accept yourself exactly as you are, but never stop trying to learn and grow. One without the other just doesn't cut it. The first, by itself, leads to complacency, the second to self-flagellation. The paradoxical trick is to embrace these opposites, using self-acceptance as an antidote to fear and as a cushion in the face of setbacks.

8. Meaning isn't something you discover; it's something you create, one step at a time. Meaning is derived from finding a way to express your unique skills and passion in the service of something larger than yourself. Figuring out how best to contribute is a lifelong challenge, reborn every day.

9. You can't change what you don't notice, and not noticing won't make it go away. Each of us has an infinite capacity for self-deception. To avoid pain, we rationalize, minimize, deny, and go numb. The antidote is the willingness

to look at yourself with unsparing honesty and to hold yourself accountable to the person you want to be.

10. When in doubt, take responsibility. It's called being an adult.

Planning effectively for entrepreneurial thinking requires Ms. Toffler and every other math teacher in grades 5-9 to dance as effectively from part to whole as from whole to part. This means we must gather pertinent documents/performance data ahead of time. *This is where the digital two-step applies to planning.*

Anyone who's responsible for carrying out the problem solving process can use digital technology to call up multiple pieces of information: individual and group performance data, unit outcomes, concept summaries, sample problems, etc. The T-S Nexus software not only makes this possible; it allows teams to project and manipulate information so they can create common assignments and assessments as well as differentiated assignments. This allows teachers to leverage their time and effort toward problem solving as a team rather individually gathering materials and organizing data.

Collaborative planning times need to be regularly scheduled and follow routines that teachers can depend on. Ms. Toffler's department chair or team leader needs to formulate critical questions to guide meeting discussions—questions that lead to a decisions and ultimately to a plan of action. Although multiple topics may be involved, the planning sessions should have a primary focus: data analysis, content planning, instructional planning, thinking strategies, etc.

Finally, it's important to retain notes from these planning sessions and to establish timelines. Lieberman and Grolnick (1997) suggest that Ms. Toffler and her colleagues need to have a shared purpose, have equal access to information, be prepared to collaborate and reflect on multiple sources of data, and be confident in the person leading the planning session to model the openness, integrity, and authenticity required to promote a sense efficacy.

The purpose of a feedback and planning cycle is to manage self efficacy as a part of the instructional process. Many people who can organize strategic (big picture) responsibilities effectively may not be effective at identifying implementation details (logistics). Theorists are often poor classroom managers. People who can make tough decisions on the run can also wreak emotional havoc on sensitive colleagues. People who are capable of motivating others often do so by avoiding tough decisions.

Optimal conditions for self efficacy are created when teachers design learning experiences to make optimal performance manageable. Collaboration among teachers requires more than a free flow of information. It requires a different kind of flow that's difficult to manage and sustain without appropriate technology.

Achieving Optimal Performance

Self efficacy isn't something that you either have or don't have. It's not something you learn as a child and never lose as an adult. As situations change (as with Ms. Toffler's life changing divorce or her students' middle school experience), so does our sense of self efficacy. It's important to recognize that seven in ten teachers are effective managers. But it's also important to recognize the difficulty of maintaining optimal performance across every learning situation.

According to Gallup surveys, 77 percent of adults in the US think learning is a matter of managing deficits (Rath 2007). Now it becomes clear that the transformation to critical thinking and self efficacy requires more than a well managed professional development process. It requires teachers and parents, businesspeople and politicians to change their attitudes and beliefs about learning

After studying optimal performance across multiple venues, Csikszentmihalyi (1990) concluded that there were several common elements present in all mastery experiences. He summarized these elements as follows:

1. A reasonable chance of completing the task successfully

2. An ability to concentrate on what we're doing

3. Clear goals

4. Immediate feedback

5. A sense of control over our actions

6. An involvement in the task that overshadows the worries and frustrations of everyday life

7. A temporary submerging of self consciousness during the experience and an emergence of heightened self esteem following it

8. The awareness of time is overshadowed by the engagement in the experience

Figure 5.2 suggests several steps Ms. Toffler and her colleagues can take in planning for the middle school math dance. These steps prepare them, to the degree possible, to compensate for their own, as well as their students', missteps on the mathematics dance floor.

Figure 5.2

Planning for Teaching Efficacy

- ✓ Teams record agendas and minutes of key decisions, people responsible for follow up, and future topics.
- ✓ Minutes are posted and used to monitor progress.
- ✓ Data is collected to determine the effectiveness of tier 1 strategies.
- ✓ Decision points are established to determine the differences between pre- and post-intervention results.
- ✓ Progress is monitored at specified time intervals to give staff the support they need to determine the effectiveness of the interventions used.

Ms. Toffler and her colleagues don't need to be experts at every dance to become entrepreneurs. Once they commit to being accountable for their combined success, it will become easier for them to replicate Csikszentmihalyi's conditions for optimal performance in all their planning meetings. Let's take a moment to look at three types of planning meetings in terms of these conditions.

Content Planning and Entrepreneurial Thinking

State curriculum frameworks and Common Core standards establish the content expectations for most states. Content planning should focus on how teachers address these expectations.

To address content planning in terms of Csikszentmihalyi's conditions for optimal performance, teachers might focus on a list of sample test items with correct responses identified. Since participants know the correct answer, they aren't distracted by the worry of answering the question incorrectly in front of their peers. Everyone has a reasonable chance of completing the task successfully, because responses are designed to elicit possible explanations rather than specific answers.

By managing the risks related to answering a question incorrectly in front of their peers, everyone can relax and concentrate on critical thinking. Because this is a collaborative planning session, participants need assurance that their ideas have value. In this way, the time and energy involved in planning is overshadowed by their engagement in a meaningful experience.

Ms. Toffler and her colleagues might consider why a particular item response is correct as well as why the other responses are not. With this material and advanced thinking in hand, content planning meetings can be focused on what Covey (1989) calls beginning with the end in mind. After agreeing on what success looks like, Ms. Toffler and her colleagues can engage in the following:

- ✓ Justifying a logical rationale for test responses (if not multiple choice, determine a rubric for required information that demonstrates basic, proficient, and advanced performance)

- ✓ Creating a pacing guide outlining when and how major concepts might be taught

- ✓ Analyzing materials for relevance, level appropriateness, accessibility, and interest

- ✓ Organizing materials and scheduling usage/rotation of computers and materials as necessary

- ✓ Assigning one or more persons to explore (Internet search) content presentations/activities to meet the needs of different learners

- ✓ Identifying material and professional development needs for future budget considerations

INSTRUCTIONAL PLANNING AND ENTREPRENEURIAL THINKING

Professional learning communities (PLCs) develop successful instructional strategies based on performance results. They study research and share best practices. Prior to a PLC meeting, Ms. Toffler's department chair might distribute an article related to a current instructional question, ask participants to identify their own successful strategies (eventually including lesson videos), or discuss findings from other planning meetings. PLC meetings should provide the following:

- ✓ Analysis of what makes instruction effective—teaching toward a clear focus, clearly stated expectations, consistent routines, effective use of class time, effective questioning, effective grouping strategies, effective summaries, laughter and student engagement, etc.

- ✓ Group review and analysis of recorded model lessons

- ✓ Anticipating when and how different learners may struggle with unit concepts

- ✓ Sharing personal instructional strengths and challenges

- ✓ Setting a focus and expectations for high leverage professional development

- ✓ Establishing timelines and logistics for peer observations and administrator observations

Since all planning should enhance critical thinking, professional development might include studying and modeling Paul and Elder's elements and clarifying questions for critical thinking, thinking maps, a think aloud, etc. Ms. Toffler and her colleagues should analyze what makes their instruction effective by thinking about the questions being asked in their classrooms and about who is asking them. They might consider the following:

- Levels of questions from teacher to students; from students to teacher; from student to student

- Use of thinking maps by teacher; by students

- Levels of thinking required on homework; on tests

It's also important to note that not all learning issues have an academic cause. Planning for nonacademic issues might include data on attendance, discipline, and student interests. This information may provide a background for determining the factors underlying students' academic struggles.

Data Analysis and Entrepreneurial Thinking

Data teams ensure that data shapes change. To prepare for a data team meeting, Ms. Toffler's department chair might prepare a brief summary of data relative to a critical question(s).

It's important to remind participants that data doesn't always need to mean a test score. It may relate to assessment, attendance, discipline, or numerous other factors related to students' learning and well being. Ms. Toffler and her colleagues might prepare for a data team meeting by engaging in the following:

- ✓ Critiquing or responding to a summary of trend data

- ✓ Gathering examples of successful practices (with data backup) relative to a specific goal or strategy

- ✓ Developing critical questions relating the data to content, instruction, critical thinking, and self efficacy decisions

With this material and thinking in hand, data team meetings will be more focused and productive. They should allow for the following:

- ✓ Identifying specific trends/needs (with test-related/goal-related rationales) to improve students' ability to manage their own learning

- ✓ Identifying teachers and students whose results indicate they need assistance

- ✓ Reviewing internal assessments for consistency with external assessments

- ✓ Creating team assessments that encourage an appropriate depth of knowledge

- ✓ Developing action plans with specific responsibilities and timelines

SUSTAINING A CULTURE OF CRITICAL THINKING AND SELF EFFICACY

Do all good teachers teach critical thinking? *Not exactly*—good teaching can't be defined by any single talent or attribute. So are you thinking, "If good teaching isn't a matter of teaching critical thinking, how will my principal evaluate my teaching? How will we evaluate and support an entrepreneurial culture throughout our school?"

In the next chapter, we'll consider the expectations that entrepreneurial thinking places on Mr. Chang and his superintendent by exploring the following questions:

1. Can we develop a culture that balances individual and systemic needs?

2. What management structures promote critical thinking and self efficacy for different temperaments?

3. Can teachers and school administrators learn to manage their own temperament strengths and liabilities as a

means of modeling multiple problem solving protocols for students?

4. How can school leaders use digital technology to bridge the gap between good intentions and effective leadership?

Producing a Dance Culture

Can We Evaluate Entrepreneurial Thinking?

It isn't easy to balance the individual and systemic needs of a school. The principal's primary responsibility is to manage the school culture in ways that promote student achievement and well being. We like to say effective principals create a positive culture, but no single person creates the culture of an organization. School cultures emerge from habits and beliefs that successful adults think contributed to their success. Entrepreneurial thinking challenges those assumptions.

In the beginning, school leaders like Mr. Chang are judged by their intentions. In the end, they're judged by their results. And there's no single set of standards they can use to monitor their performance along the way. There are multiple sets: Common Core standards, community standards, staff standards, etc. That's why Mr. Chang says, "My job as principal is to protect my teachers from the wolves—the parents and central office folks." Like every principal, Mr. Chang knows his success depends on his teachers' success.

But Mr. Chang's leadership dance isn't always logical or sequential. He spends months building teachers and parents' support for a new math project, only to have his plans diminished by budget cutbacks.

 Now I'm trying to figure out the best way to let teachers know they won't be receiving their new math materials this year and their team planning time has been reduced to save dollars.

One of Mr. Chang's biggest challenges is managing expectations. That's why principals are encouraged to include representatives from various stakeholder groups in the school's decision making process. Some states even require principals to have advisory committees composed of students, parents, teachers, and community members. While these advisory groups span diverse roles, they ignore the differences in how people within each of these groups process information and events within their daily lives.

Temperament characteristics affect people's attitudes about change regardless of their age or group. Idealist/Blues value solutions that honor connections among people—solutions that promote harmony and personal expression. Guardian/Golds value solutions that are realistic and manageable—solutions that limit significant changes to established procedures. Rational/Greens value solutions based on sound reasoning—solutions that are consistent with the school's mission. Artisan/Oranges value solutions that allow room for the unexpected—solutions that allow a degree of spontaneity and originality.

So, the thinking goes, if we include enough stakeholders on our advisory group, we should get a cross section of opinions, right? You guessed it—*not exactly*. Guardian/ Golds are more likely than any other temperament group to participate on standing committees. Idealist/Blues may show up for meetings, but they'll usually sit quietly to avoid creating tension. Rational/Greens avoid most committees because they see them as political action groups rather than groups of rational problem solvers. Artisan/Oranges show up en masse when they think they can influence specific issues.

Managing a culture requires more than a commitment to a common vision and a willingness to engage multiple stakeholder groups in decision making. Leaders like Mr. Chang have to look beyond their stakeholders' obvious differences like roles and age to see the thinking that drives their decision making. Mr. Chang can use temperament to make certain his advisory group truly represents a cross section of his community's thinking.

Change doesn't wait for the perfect alignment of talents and circumstances, and Mr. Chang can't control circumstances. But he can manage talents. He can't allow changing circumstances to distract him from transforming talents into strengths.

Budget increases and budget cuts are temporary at best. Textbooks and technology change with regularity. Individuals come and go. Mr. Chang may have come to the dance expecting to cha-cha. The question is, "Can he improvise if the band's playing a salsa?" If Mr. Chang is to become a transformational leader, he has to become what I call a *principled opportunist*. Principled opportunists are anchored in a core set of research-based, reality-tested, child-centered principles, but they remain alert for the right opportunity to advance their core values.

Transformational leaders recognize that most teachers and most school leaders (65 to 70 percent) are uncomfortable with change. They know that the school culture will choose

> *If Mr. Chang is to become a transformational leader, he has to become a principled opportunist.*

consistency over logic, rules and procedures over personal feelings. They also recognize that parents want their children to be happy and successful in school; whereas, business and political leaders want those same children to develop the skills necessary to sustain the nation's economic and political engine.

Managing Critical Thinking and Self Efficacy

Mastering content isn't the purpose of education. The purpose is for students to build the capacity to manage their own learning. Common Core standards provide the parameters used to measure progress. Critical thinking ensures that our actions match our words. Mastery experiences create pathways to self-efficacy.

Change is an Artisan/Orange process. It requires adapting behaviors to fit new circumstances. But change makes many people uncomfortable. It violates the Idealist/Blue need for harmony and the Guardian/Gold sense of consistency. Sometimes change occurs before people have all the data necessary to answer every Rational/Green question.

Mr. Chang can't address every stakeholder's specific concerns or disappointments. But he can address patterns of concern that cut across all groups. Figure 6.1 shows how he can manage the key interests of Idealist, Guardian, Rational, and Artisan stakeholders.

Figure 6.1

The Four-Ps of a Quality Transformation

	POINT A	SPACES BETWEEN THE NOTES			POINT B
	Expectations	Questions	Classroom Realities	Planning	Results
Purpose		Why are we doing this?	To build talents into strengths through critical thinking	Managing learning to achieve multiple mastery experiences	Creating life-long learners
Parameters		How can we manage it?	Addressing content standards and performance data through digital technology	Focus meeting agendas and minutes on modifying instruction to meet individual needs	Entrepreneurial thinking across content areas
Principles		How will we monitor our progress?	Create a feedback loop focused on critical thinking and self-efficacy	Ask critical questions focused on growth in student performance	Evaluation focused on creating entrepreneurial thinkers
Priorities		Where should we start?	Use digital technology as a tier 1 instructional tool	Use digital technology to plan agendas, assignments, and assessment	Revise and digitize the evaluation process

The real advantage to this chart comes from using it before, during, and after a project. The columns from left to right represent stages in an ongoing transformation process. They begin with point A *expectations* and end with point B *results*. The *classroom realities* column represents the point at which expectations and results meet. The expectations column lists a key word to describe how different stakeholders—from top to bottom, Idealist/Blue, Guardian/Gold, Rational/Green, and Artisan/Orange—interpret success.

Mr. Chang can use the questions from column two to manage expectations. He can use the planning strategies from column four to monitor commitment.

> *A reasonable amount of risk doesn't mean everyone will always feel comfortable.*

It's important for stakeholders to agree on the general direction of a project. It's equally important for them to agree on what the midterm (classroom) and end (school wide) results could look like. But many projects fail because leaders avoid talking about and planning for the potential risks involved in getting from Point A to Point B. The path from expectations to results seldom follows a straight line.

Mr. Chang can use the questions in the second column to clarify the risks involved when expectations meet reality. Everyone knows what's possible; they just don't want to admit what's likely to happen when the ideal meets the unexpected. It's also easy to overlook the fact that stakeholder *agreement* is not the same thing as *total commitment*. Unless Mr. Chang and his staff agree on how they will monitor the project through their daily and weekly planning processes, they will not hold themselves individually and collectively accountable for school wide outcomes.

Mr. Chang's goal is to manage a *reasonable* amount of risk. A reasonable amount of risk doesn't mean everyone will always feel comfortable. Stakeholders can tolerate a degree of discomfort if it leads to a series of mastery experiences over time. Change defines a snapshot in time. Transformation defines growth over time. Change impacts preferences. Transformation emerges when people can distinguish between individual preferences and real educational needs.

Guardian/Gold stakeholders feel most comfortable knowing changes won't become a part of the school's ongoing parameters until they can be managed reasonably over time. Transformational leaders can use the Four Ps to anticipate potential obstacles and highlight them from the outset of any project. They can inspire others, not by being right or demanding that others are always right, but by charting a path through adversity. They need to accept setbacks as part of the transformation process.

Transformation requires more than a single drumbeat and an inspired drum major. Stakeholders know it's impossible for Mr. Chang to anticipate every potential obstacle or budget problem. But, as a transformational leader, he can manage a response to those events that support people through difficult times. This means improvising without compromising the fundamental principles of teaching and learning that build a school wide capacity for self efficacy.

No single factor holds the key to effective transformation. Schools exist within an environment of constant flux. The world didn't become flat (Friedman 2004) in a day or a year. Deep change

(Quinn 1996) involves personality factors that reach beyond words and behaviors to capture attitudes and beliefs. Having the right people on the bus (Peters 1989) doesn't mean having people that agree with everything the leader proposes. *Transformational leaders live by a definition of leadership that transcends doing things right if it allows them to do the right things* (Bennis 1989).

Education reform stars are seldom perfectly aligned, but we can't afford a reform model focused on deficits. In that model, Guardian/Gold reformers fill the deficits with more rules, more uniformity, and good old-fashioned direct teaching. Idealist/Blue reformers fill the deficits with more parent involvement, more community service, and life as art. Rational/Green reformers fill them with more questions, more STEM classes, and higher order thinking. Artisan/Oranges look for quick fixes: more online education, more privatization of school services, and merit pay. All these roads are paved with good intentions, but all lead to the same place.

Transformational leaders work in a world that's results focused but habit driven. This is a world where ethics and logic define our rules but immediate events drive our actions. This is a world where it's easier to *agree* on the nature of general project outcomes than to *commit* to the level of individual and group pain required to reach those outcomes.

> *Transformational leaders work in a world that's results focused but habit driven.*

Mr. Chang is a producer. Tom, Lakya, Juan, and Jamal each show up for middle school ready to dance—to engage in learning.

Because they're only aspiring dancers at this point, they need an experienced dance instructor like Ms. Toffler to model the dance and to provide authentic feedback regarding their moves. But remember, Ms. Toffler is only one of several dance instructors at the school. Since 65 to 70 percent of these teachers are Guardian/Gold, it's not hard to convince them what needs to happen. If they just had a bit more time and cooperation from the parents and district office administrators, they could repair those deficits in students' thinking, right?

Not exactly—Mr. Chang has to deal with a Blue/Idealist art teacher who never reads her e-mail. He has to deal with a Rational/Green science teacher who is so abrasive that other staff members avoid him. He has to deal with an Artisan/Orange coach who spends much more time focusing on high school basketball than on middle school social studies. He also has to remember that several of his teachers have strong personal ties to the community that outweigh their performance in the classroom. Parents and community members also have multiple definitions of what success looks like. They often credit or blame the schools for the degree of success they've experienced in their lives. *Welcome to the dance.*

The Leadership Dance—I've got Your Back

Can teachers and school administrators learn to manage their own temperament strengths and liabilities as a means of modeling multiple problem solving protocols for students?

Can We Evaluate Entrepreneurial Thinking?

Tom, Lakya, Juan, and Jamal have the ability to exercise mathematical reasoning. But they need help—first in recognizing where their math talents lie and then in strengthening those talents by learning to manage, rather than trying to eliminate, every math deficit.

Mr. Chang's job requires that he knows Ms. Toffler and her colleagues well enough to recognize their instructional talents. He needs to produce a school culture that leverages his staff's collective talents to bridge their individual deficits.

> Mr. Chang...needs to produce a school culture that leverages his staff's collective talents to bridge their individual deficits.

Since 65 to 70 percent of his teachers are effective managers, Mr. Chang can capitalize on their management strengths. But he's responsible for producing a dance that ensures all students become proficient dancers. Rather than having all teachers focus on a sequential set of single topic workshops, he can create groups of experts on multiple topics: content, instruction, critical thinking, and self efficacy, along with web surfers who will scan the Internet for current topics to capture students' interest across content areas.

Mr. Chang can rely on some teachers to manage routines and procedures that address state curriculum frameworks and Common Core standards. He can rely on others to manage a schedule that enhances flexible and creative student grouping. He can establish a series of teams that meet at specific times to analyze data, reflect on instructional practices, and share responsibilities for monitoring and motivating students based on their unique skill sets.

As a transformational leader, Mr. Chang can encourage entrepreneurial thinking by asking critical questions like those listed in figure 6.2.

Figure 6.2
Critical Leadership Questions

- What was the purpose of that strategy in terms of student achievement and well-being?
- How did we implement the strategy, and what materials did we use?
- How did we evaluate student performance?
- What evidence do we have to validate our evaluation of the strategy?
- Does our evidence address critical thinking and self efficacy?
- Does our evidence include qualitative student feedback?
- How will we collaborate with colleagues to plan next steps?
- What is our timeline?
- How can we support one another in making these adjustments?

Mr. Chang can make certain that all meetings align teaching and leadership responsibilities around four key structures: content, instruction, critical thinking, and self efficacy. He can remind teachers and ask them to remind him that the ultimate goal of their work is to develop entrepreneurial thinkers—to help students dance in the spaces between the notes.

School leaders are more effective when they work with people who can work as a team. We can't control events, but we can manage meetings to address events in a manner that's consistent with our systemic purpose. We can help team members make effective decisions by keeping them focused on the right critical questions. The answers to these critical questions about entrepreneurial thinking shape the leadership dance in the spaces between the notes.

Effective teams share responsibilities. They meet in subgroups that develop expertise in content, instruction, assessment, and professional development. They develop user friendly electronic meeting agendas and minutes. They rely on leaders to review minutes regularly, to identify challenges to the transformation process, and to develop strategies to address these challenges. They address content planning and curriculum alignment, instruction, critical thinking, and logistics.

Some of Mr. Chang's teachers (25 to 35 percent) are like Juan—Idealist/Blue. They're hesitant to organize, analyze, and act on their own. Mr. Chang will need to appreciate their sensitivities: their fear of embarrassment when their actions violate written or unwritten norms, their fear of missing a key step in an instructional sequence, their need to avoid *dumb* questions. He knows that decision making requires a degree of Artisan/Orange risk taking. But he'll manage those risks through pilots that include planning, analysis, and refinement stages.

Mr. Chang knows no single group of stakeholders, regardless of their temperament or life experiences, controls the outcome of this middle school dance. It's easier to do things right by appeasing people's Guardian/Gold expectations, especially since they probably represent 65 to 70 percent of his teaching staff and 40 to 45% of his community. But transformational leaders don't settle for doing things right. They assume the risks of doing the right things.

Guardian/Gold teachers need to know the rules before they take a risk. These teachers value what the system evaluates. That's why Mr. Chang focuses his evaluations on the values expressed in figure 6.3, values that address the spaces between the expectations of point A and the results of point B.

Figure 6.3

	Teaching Performance Indicators
1 Content Planning	Lesson objective aligns with pacing guide. Materials are grade-level appropriate and organized for effective use. Materials are differentiated for performance levels and learning styles.
2 Instructional Planning	Subject matter is current or related to a current example. Teacher states objective(s) in terms of student performance. Teacher models problem solving protocols. Students practice problem solving protocols with teacher guidance. Students practice problem solving protocols independently as teacher monitors.
3 Critical thinking	Students summarize key steps in problem solving protocols. Teacher models critical thinking through one or more of the following: think-aloud, RUBIES, thinking map, critical questions, other_____. Students model critical thinking through one or more of the following: think-aloud, RUBIES, thinking map, critical questions, ther_____ with teacher guidance. Students model critical thinking through one or more of the following: think-aloud, RUBIES, thinking map, critical questions, other_____ as teacher monitors.
4 Data-Driven Decision Making (Efficacy)	Teacher identifies individual/group performance relative to expected performance and models growth strategies (analysis of desired versus actual performance, identification of breakdowns in reasoning, goal setting with timeline, analysis of results). Teacher guides students through a comparison of pre-intervention performance with post-intervention performance. Students identify their performance relative to expected performance and set growth goals. Students articulate specific growth strategies relative to practice/intervention activities. Students compare pre-intervention performance to post-intervention performance as teacher monitors.

These criteria help teachers like Ms. Toffler and her math colleagues focus on how their planning logistics enhance the talents (temperament) that students like Tom, Lakya, Juan, and Jamal bring to the table. Mr. Chang will develop credibility with his stakeholders by acknowledging his own mistakes as well as their successes. He'll help stakeholders harmonize respect for ideas with respect for people and data analysis with an ability to act even when all the data may not be available. He'll urge them to accept existing routines and procedures until better ones can be developed and managed.

A talent for organization and hard work can become a curse unless it allows for reasonable risks. Guardian/Golds can harmonize their talent for organization with their need to take risks, their talent for following directions with their need to question assumptions, their willingness to delay gratification with their need to appreciate the people and events of the moment.

Mr. Chang and all transformational leaders can use technology to build talents into strengths. They can digitize meeting agendas and minutes, evaluation forms, and numerous other documents so they're readily available for daily use. Transformational leaders can use the procedures listed below to build their staff's capacity for reflective practice.

- ✓ Using a pre-observation form that asks teachers to identify what they're teaching, encourages them to identify instructional strategies that they're trying to perfect, and allows them to indicate the kind of feedback they find most beneficial for growth.

- ✓ Following the observation with a half-page summary of the teacher's purpose for the observation along with non-judgmental observations from the class.

- ✓ On the second half of this single page, ask teachers three to five critical (nonjudgmental) questions that focus on the reasoning behind their instructional decisions.

- ✓ Consistently asking teachers to provide oral or written evidence to support their decision-making strategies.

- ✓ Helping teachers set personal goals and encouraging them to engage in conversations with their colleagues to identify a common focus for curriculum alignment, data team, and professional learning community meetings.

Mr. Chang can use these steps to build a culture of critical thinking that supports and sustains entrepreneurial thinking throughout the school. Digital technology won't decrease Ms. Toffler's workload. But it can shift the focus of that workload from content and assessment to critical thinking and self efficacy.

The first step in making this transformation requires a significant shift in existing attitudes and beliefs about teaching and learning. In any profession, people have to overcome old habits in order to embrace new routines and procedures that promote entrepreneurial thinking. This requires Mr. Chang and his teachers to support one another until critical thinking and self efficacy become embedded in the overall school culture.

Mr. Chang's position as a middle school principal can be lonely at times—especially in times of significant change. As he and other transformational leaders attempt to lead the dance beyond an idea, a strategy, or a plan, they need someone to support them. This *I've got your back* leadership falls to district office administrators. Without it, what started out as a dance in the spaces between the notes will quickly collapse into one more lockstep march.

The Leadership Dance—Who Has My Back?

Mr. Chang's task as the producer is to get teachers, parents, and district office administrators to support a transformation process in his middle school. This requires a significant risk. The biggest risk for Mr. Chang is that he has to transform his own leadership values and beliefs. He has to model transformative thinking in his day to day conversations with parents and teachers.

Mr. Chang knows students who master algebra will be prepared for the parade toward college and a STEM career—if that is the path they choose to pursue. But he also knows he can't assume students who haven't mastered algebra according to the established timeline should simply be sent to the practice area for remediation or guided toward the sidewalk so they won't interfere with the parade.

He won't make a formal transformation proposal to his superintendent without consulting with teachers and parents. But he knows he has to lead this transformation. He'll share his stakeholders' dreams as well as their concerns with the superintendent. Then he'll make an offer his superintendent can't refuse. He'll share his plan to create multiple mastery experiences that will increase his students' odds of meeting the school district's graduation requirements. He'll also explain how this will prepare them for success in a STEM driven world. His plan will address the following:

Mastery experience	Specific growth goals for student achievement
Social modeling	Description of what the transformation involves in terms of time and dollars
Social persuasion	Assurance that there are reasonable backup plans to support stakeholders under pressure
Psychological response	Reasonable timelines that have staff and community support

Mr. Chang will ask the superintendent to cover his back by holding him accountable for not only doing things right, but also for doing the right things: meeting criteria such as those listed in figure 6.4.

Figure 6.4

	Leadership Performance Indicators
1 Content Planning	Agendas/minutes address pacing guides and are consistent with yearly action plan.
	Meeting materials include evidence of effective content planning.
	Materials address differentiation for performance levels and learning styles.
	Discussions address students' needs and facilitate instructional management.
	Administrative conferences/summaries address content topics from meetings/PLCs.
2 Instructional Planning	Agendas/minutes address thinking levels consistent with yearly action plan.
	Meeting materials provide evidence of effective instructional planning.
	Sample lessons encourage peer and supervisory feedback.
	Teachers practice problem solving protocols in the classroom with peer and administrator modeling, feedback, and support.
	Administrative conferences/summaries identify and/or address instructional topics from meetings/PLCs and performance goals.
3 Critical thinking	Agendas/minutes address critical thinking through think-aloud, RUBIES, thinking map, critical questions, other_____ consistent with yearly action plan.
	PLCs model critical thinking through reflection on one or more of the following: think-aloud, RUBIES, thinking map, critical questions, other_____.
	Sample lessons are analyzed and discussed to encourage peer and supervisory feedback relative to critical thinking.
	Administrative conferences/summaries address critical thinking topics from meetings/PLCs and are consistent with the yearly action plan.
4 Data-Driven Decision Making (Efficacy)	Agendas/minutes address individual/group performance relative to expected performance (reasoning, goal setting with timeline, analysis of results).
	Lesson/unit plans show evidence of decisions to change curriculum and/or instructional strategies (grouping, differentiated assignments, etc.) based on analysis of student performance.
	Peers work through a comparison of pre-intervention performance with post-intervention performance (sharing observation/conference documents, videos, etc.).
	Administrative conferences/summaries address performance goals related to topics from meetings/PLCs.

Transformational leaders like Mr. Chang will use these criteria as guidelines for ongoing conversations with students, teachers, and parents—conversations that maintain their commitment to entrepreneurial thinking. Such conversations not only clarify the vision for stakeholders. They clarify the line of demarcation between short-term change and sustainable transformation. We can't control entrepreneurial outcomes, but we can evaluate multiple aspects of entrepreneurial thinking: content, instruction, critical thinking, and self efficacy. Transformational leaders understand that changing behaviors isn't enough to sustain meaningful change. Transformation requires a shift at a deeper level involving values and beliefs. It involves an ongoing process of dancing in the spaces between the notes.

Conclusion

Educating students for entrepreneurial thinking doesn't mean every student will become a small-business owner. It means they'll learn to organize, manage, and assume risks for their own learning. They'll learn to see patterns, to make connections, to work as members of a team, and to make sense of the changes that impact their daily lives. We can define entrepreneurial thinking. But as educators, we need to explore what it looks like from the classroom to the boardroom. *We need to create a school culture that creates entrepreneurial thinkers.*

As students enter adolescence, their brains develop connections that enable them to think critically beyond the level of personal experience. These new connections accentuate the chasm between their existing knowledge base and what they're capable of learning. The role of the middle school teacher is to help students bridge this gap.

More often than not, we slow the traffic on that bridge by using digital technology to increase the flow of information and the amount of practice time spent on memorization and mimicry. This march works for a career on an assembly line, but it doesn't prepare students for success in a world where new information challenges our assumptions on a daily basis. Digital technology can indicate what students know and don't know, but it takes a teacher to shape practice activities that promote lifelong learning. Teachers can use technology to manage content, instructional planning, and assessment routines so they have more time to focus on developing critical thinking and self efficacy.

The transformation from assembly-line practice to entrepreneurial thinking requires more than a shift in what we do and how long we take to do it. It requires a shift in *our* thinking. If we function as though learning is simply a product of more content and more practice, we won't leverage technology to transform the way we teach. Technology can be more than an intervention tool or a digital babysitter. It can become a tier I management tool that increases opportunities for critical thinking and innovation in our classrooms.

Throughout this book we've questioned several assumptions about learning based on a logical sequential march from point A to point B. Learning involves more than Common Core standards and standardized tests. It requires an ability to accept that things aren't always right or wrong. We have to teach students to dance in the spaces between right and wrong. Critical thinking and self efficacy provide students with the tools necessary to distinguish between qualitative and quantitative differences. This is the dance that inspires *intellectual productivity*.

On the basis of my thirty-eight years as a teacher, site administrator, and superintendent, I am suggesting that *the logical sequential assumptions driving our daily educational practices are destroying the entrepreneurial thinking that has made the US a beacon of hope for creating a more democratic world.* Students like Tom, Lakya, Juan, and Jamal can achieve mastery experiences in math. But first, we have to debunk some of the fundamental assumptions driving the risk-averse culture in which educators like Ms. Toffler and Mr. Chang find themselves.

Being smart is not exactly a matter of DNA

Students won't learn to organize, manage, and assume the risks of entrepreneurial thinking until they develop an understanding of how they think. As long as educators focus on learning as a form of mimicry, Tom and most of his teachers will continue to *dance* on the Guardian/Gold, risk-averse portion of the dance floor. Waiting for specific directions from an authority figure is a means of avoiding risk. *Tom needs to practice managing risks.*

Juan limits his dance to the Idealist/Blue portion of the floor. His empathy for others clouds his need to make sense of the world as it is so he can pursue his dreams of what it could become. *Juan won't gain anything from practice until the classroom becomes a safe place for him to make mistakes.*

Lakya's brain is wired for reflection. She's so familiar with the Rational/Green portion of the dance floor that she assumes critical thinking will make up for her lack of practice and self-discipline. *She needs to practice turning her ideas into a meaningful intellectual product by setting realistic goals and timelines.*

Jamal's brain is wired for risk taking. He's so busy experiencing every aspect of his Artisan/Orange world that he overlooks how those experiences are connected. *He needs to practice setting short term benchmarks that allow him to reflect on his experiences as he goes. He needs to practice slowing down enough to monitor and adjust his efforts (successes and mistakes) toward longer term goals.*

Practice doesn't exactly make perfect

Practicing the right things makes perfect. We can use Paul and Elder's critical thinking standards to help all students pose critical questions in a respectful manner that promotes entrepreneurial thinking. We can encourage students to think aloud through complex content so entrepreneurial thinking becomes a part of their daily classroom activities. When thinking becomes visible, we can help students analyze and improve it.

As educators, we spend so much time managing content that we leave little time for students to reflect on their own learning. Critical thinking doesn't eliminate the risks involved with learning. It helps individuals manage those risks. If we let students like Tom and Lakya carry classroom discussions, their *correct* responses prevent others from conducting their own critical analyses. The fact that Juan and Jamal can mimic Tom and Lakya's answers doesn't guarantee they can replicate their thinking.

Critical thinking isn't exactly the key to success

Self efficacy comes from experiencing mastery under multiple circumstances. Daily problems don't always have a single answer. Similar student responses don't always indicate a similar understanding of key concepts. Conditions change and expectations change.

We can use Bandura's sources of self efficacy to structure mastery experiences that help all students understand how to adapt their thinking in order to manage it across multiple situations. We can engage authentically with students by being empathetic instead of sympathetic. That is, we can help them recognize their deficits as obstacles to be overcome rather than excuses for giving up.

Thinking skills are not exactly more important than content

Sixty-five to seventy percent of educators dance on the Guardian/Gold portion of the dance floor. Forty-five to fifty percent of our students dance there with them. These individuals don't manage risk. They avoid it. They feel safer asking for a specific response than asking a critical question that allows for multiple responses. The problem is that the rest of the world is dancing somewhere else.

Teachers can use digital technology to organize content, planning, and assessment that turn students' innate talents into academic strengths. That academic success can lead to a salable intellectual product for a global marketplace. We can use technology to reach back for missing information and skills and incorporate them within current grade level expectations. We can *reach back* and *teach forward.*

Self efficacy comes from managing risks in order to explore possibilities across all areas of the dance floor—across all content areas. It comes from mastering our moods, emotional states, physical reactions, and stress levels so we can solve complex problems outside our comfort zone. Digital technology can help us manage some of the risks associated with entrepreneurial thinking.

Good teachers don't always teach critical thinking

All teachers can teach critical thinking. But first, they have to become more effective critical thinkers themselves. The Common Core standards for math require critical thinking and self efficacy, not simply more data. Teachers are drowning in digital data.

We don't need more data to drive our decisions. We need better thinking. We need to think more about how students actually learn before we can decide the kinds of practice they need to achieve mastery. Digital technology won't guarantee that the Ms. Tofflers and Mr. Changs of this world can change every middle school overnight. Changing middle schools won't change every assumption driving education from early childhood through high school graduation. But we can begin the transformation. US schools can become entrepreneurial centers where students learn to function successfully in a democracy. Students who learn to manage information are more likely to be successful in school. Students who learn to manage their own learning have a better chance of being successful in life.

We can't evaluate entrepreneurial thinking through test scores

Entrepreneurial thinking does not exclude test scores. It requires using test data to make effective decisions about teaching and learning. It involves using critical thinking to manage risks. Educators are effective managers. We need to build on those innate strengths to organize, manage, and assume the risks associated with teaching in a democracy. We need to become educational entrepreneurs.

Students won't experience mastery unless our evaluations of students and staff are designed to assess it. If we value entrepreneurial thinking, we need to find better ways to evaluate it from the classroom to the boardroom. Our evaluations need to address the Four Ps:

Purpose	Why are we doing this?
Parameters	How can we manage it?
Principles	How will we monitor our progress?
Priorities	Where should we start?

Change is a snapshot in time. Transformation is a dance produced over time, a dance that transcends genetics and socioeconomic levels. The transformation from a lockstep march to an entrepreneurial dance may differ between Chicago's North Shore and Mississippi's small rural towns. The dance of a poor African American or Hispanic community may not mirror that of a white, middle-class community. But the principles of critical thinking and self efficacy described in this book can be used to transform the way we think about learning and teaching. We don't need textbooks and software developers to fix people. We need them to help us build bridges that transform individual talents into systemic strengths. *The future of education lies in these spaces between the notes.*

Resources

A List of Resources and Sample Tools by Chapter

Chapter 1

For more information on temperament, consider the following:

    www.realcolors.org

    www.keirsey.com

Chapter 2

For more information on critical thinking, consider the following:

    www.criticalthinking.net

    www.inspiration.com

Chapter 3

For more information on self efficacy, consider the following:

    www.emory.edu

Chapter 4

For more information on T-S Nexus, consider the following:

    http://tsn-world.neoedu.net

Chapter 5

For planning and meeting formats and digital planning tools, consider the following:

    www.mccomb.k12.ms.us

    www.k12els.com

Chapter 6

For more information on building leadership capacity and digital evaluation, consider the following:

    www.triplec21.com

    www.k12els.com

References

Bandura, A. 1977. *Social Learning Theory.* New York: General Learning Press.

———. 1997. *Self efficacy: The Exercise of Control.* New York: W. H. Freeman.

Bennis, W. 1989. *On Becoming a Leader.* Reading, Mass.: Addison-Wesley.

Brookes, D. 2011. *The Social Animal: The Hidden Sources of Love, Character, and Achievement.* New York: Random House.

Cashman, K. 2008. *Leadership from the Inside Out: Becoming a Leader for Life.* San Francisco: Berrett-Koehler.

Covey, S. 1989. *The Seven Habits of Highly Effective People: Restoring the Character Ethic.* New York: Simon and Schuster.

Csikszentmihalyi, M. 1990. *Flow: The Psychology of Optimal Experience.* New York: Harper & Row.

Freidman, T. 1989. *The World Is Flat: A Brief History of the Twenty-first Century.* New York: Picador.

Johnson, D. 2004. *The Real Colors Homeowner's Guide.* Phoenix: National Curriculum and Training Institute.

———. 2005. *Real Relationships.* Phoenix: National Curriculum and Training Institute, 2005.

———. 2005. *Real Parenting.* Phoenix: National Curriculum and Training Institute.

———. 2005. *Sustaining Change in Schools.* Arlington, Va.: Association for supervision and Curriculum Development.

Keirsey D. and Bates, M. 1998. *Please Understand Me II: Temperament, Character, Intelligence.* Del Mar, Calif.: Prometheus Nemesis Books.

Lehrer, J. 2012. *Imagine: How Creativity Works.* New York: Houghton Mifflin Harcourt.

Levine, M. 2002. *A Mind at a Time.* New York: Simon and Schuster.

Paul, R. and Elder, L. 2002. *Critical Thinking: Tools for Taking Charge of your Personal and Professional Life.* Upper Saddle River, N.J.: Prentice-Hall.

REFERENCES

Peters, T. and Austin, N. 1989. *A Passion for Excellence: The Leadership Difference.* New York: Warner Books.

Quinn, R. 1996. *Deep Change.* San Francisco: Jossey-Bass.

———. 2004. *Building the Bridge as You Walk on It.* San Francisco: Jossey-Bass.

Rath, T. 2007. *Strengths Finder 2.0.* New York: Gallup Press.

Schwartz, T., Gomes, J., and McCarthy, C. 2011. *Be Excellent at Anything: The Four Keys to Transforming the Way We Work and Live.* New York: Free Press.

Taylor, J.B.T. 2006. *My Stroke of Insight: A Brain Scientist's Personal Journey.* New York: Viking.

Thinking Maps. 2010. www.thinkingmaps.com.

Trends in Mathematics and Science Study. 2007-2011. http://nces.ed.gov/timss/.

TS-Nexus as a Mathematics Evaluation System Software. 2003. Seoul: Korean Institute of Curriculum and Evaluation.

Wilhelm, J. 2001. "Think alouds make invisible mental processes visible to children." *Instructor:* 2001 v111, pp. 26-28.

Index

Abstract random, 27
Accuracy, 38, 39, 49, 57
Adaptive confidence, 53
Algorithms, 21, 24, 77, 82
Artisan/Orange, 15, 16, 17, 18, 19, 34, 35, 36, 45, 46, 47, 51, 55, 72, 75, 76, 81, 88, 89, 94, 113, 115, 117, 119, 120, 123, 136
Authentic engagement, 53

Blue, see Idealist/Blue
Breadth, 38, 39
Building the bridge, 48

Clarity, 38, 39, 56, 57

Common Core, 14, 39, 43, 44, 47, 53, 59, 87, 103, 112, 115, 121, 134, 138
Content planning, 30, 99, 103, 104, 123, 125
Critical leadership questions, 122
Critical questions, 37, 38, 99, 107, 122, 127, 136, 137
Critical thinking, 14, 27, 28, 29, 31, 35, 36, 37, 38, 40, 43, 44, 45, 49, 57, 59, 61, 73, 79, 80, 83, 84, 85, 87, 88, 91, 92, 95, 101, 103, 106, 107, 108, 121, 123, 125, 127, 130, 131, 134, 136, 137, 138, 139, 140

Data team, 106, 107, 127
Deficits, 35, 40, 44, 67, 80, 81, 101, 119, 120, 121, 137
Depth, 38, 39, 56, 68, 85, 108
Detached interdependence, 55
Digital technology, 61, 62, 66, 67, 68, 73, 74, 77, 80, 84, 99, 109, 127, 134, 137, 138
Digital two-step, 77, 85
DNA, 3, 20, 21, 77, 93, 135

Efficacy, 48, 49, 50, 51, 56, 57, 59, 61, 73, 79, 80, 83, 85, 89, 90, 91, 92, 94, 95, 97, 100, 101, 102, 107, 108, 115, 118, 121, 125, 127, 130 131, 134, 135, 137, 138, 140
Empathy, 31, 36, 53, 92, 93, 94, 95, 135, 137
Entrepreneur, 26, 44, 54, 55, 56, 57, 59, 61, 65, 66, 68, 90, 91, 94, 99, 103, 105, 106, 108, 111, 112, 122, 123, 127, 131, 133, 134, 135, 136, 138, 139

Fairness, 38
Four- Ps, 116, 139

Gold, see Guardian/Gold

Guardian/Gold, 16, 17, 18, 19, 20, 21, 24, 27, 31, 32, 35, 36, 40, 45, 46, 47, 52, 55, 72, 75, 76, 80, 81, 87, 88, 89, 94, 113, 115, 117, 118, 119, 120, 124, 126, 135, 137
Gradual release, 88, 90
Green, see rational/green

Higher order thinking, 37, 39, 40

Idealist/Blue, 16, 17, 18, 19, 31, 32, 35, 36, 45, 46, 47, 52, 55, 56, 72, 75, 76, 81, 88, 89, 92, 94, 95, 113, 115, 117, 119, 120, 123, 135
Instructional planning, 39, 69, 99, 105, 134
Intellectual productivity, 135

Leadership performance indicators, 130
Logic, 38, 39
Logical sequential, 5, 6, 27, 69, 134

Managing expectations, 112
Mastery experience, 48, 49, 50, 51, 66, 91, 92, 101, 115, 117, 129, 135, 137

INDEX

Mathematical thinking, 16, 59, 74, 79

Mathematical reasoning, 27, 28, 53, 82, 84, 121

Neurological functions, 74

Optimal performance, 100, 101, 103,

Orange, see artisan/orange

Parameters, 94, 115, 116, 117, 139

Personal growth plan, 60

Planning for excellence, 96

PLC, 105

Practice, 9, 18, 19, 20, 21, 22, 23, 24, 29, 31, 36, 39, 40, 44, 46, 50, 52, 69, 72, 73, 79, 89, 94, 105, 107, 121, 126, 128, 134, 135, 136, 138

Precision, 38, 39, 56, 57

Principles, 94, 96, 116, 118, 139, 140

Priorities, 116, 139

Psychological response, 49, 50, 51, 129

Purpose, 18, 30, 39, 100, 115, 116, 123, 127, 139

Rational/Green, 16, 17, 18, 19, 27, 31, 33, 35, 36, 45, 47, 51, 55, 72, 75, 76, 77, 81, 88, 89, 93, 94, 113, 115, 117, 119, 120, 136

Reach back – teach forward, 65, 77, 79, 80, 82, 83, 84, 85, 138

Reflective practice, 126

Relevance, 38, 104

Responsible freedom, 55

Self efficacy, see efficacy

Significance, 38

Social modeling, 49, 53

Social persuasion, 49, 129

Sources of Self Efficacy, 49

STEM, 128, 129

Teaching Performance Indicators, 125

Temperament, 15, 17, 44, 45, 46, 80

Temperament distribution, 17

Think aloud, 29, 30, 31, 35, 36, 37, 39, 56, 57, 72, 79, 106, 136

Thinking map, 52, 57, 58, 106

Tier 1, 69, 72, 77, 80

TIMSS, 24, 68
Tough love, 56, 57
Transformation, 89, 91, 95, 101, 114, 116, 118, 119, 122, 123, 126, 127, 129, 130, 134, 138, 139

Transformational leader, 114, 117, 118, 119, 122, 124, 126, 128, 130
T-S Nexus, 69, 70, 71, 72, 99

www.ingramcontent.com/pod-product-compliance
Lightning Source LLC
Chambersburg PA
CBHW070803100426
42742CB00012B/2237